T0222260

Data Merge and Styles for Adobe InDesign CC 2018

Creating Custom Documents for Mailouts and Presentation Packages

Jennifer Harder

Apress®

Data Merge and Styles for Adobe InDesign CC 2018

Jennifer Harder
Delta, British Columbia, Canada

ISBN-13 (pbk): 978-1-4842-3158-6   ISBN-13 (electronic): 978-1-4842-3159-3
https://doi.org/10.1007/978-1-4842-3159-3

Library of Congress Control Number: 2017959332

Copyright © 2017 by Jennifer Harder

This work is subject to copyright. All rights are reserved by the Publisher, whether the whole or part of the material is concerned, specifically the rights of translation, reprinting, reuse of illustrations, recitation, broadcasting, reproduction on microfilms or in any other physical way, and transmission or information storage and retrieval, electronic adaptation, computer software, or by similar or dissimilar methodology now known or hereafter developed.

Trademarked names, logos, and images may appear in this book. Rather than use a trademark symbol with every occurrence of a trademarked name, logo, or image we use the names, logos, and images only in an editorial fashion and to the benefit of the trademark owner, with no intention of infringement of the trademark.

The use in this publication of trade names, trademarks, service marks, and similar terms, even if they are not identified as such, is not to be taken as an expression of opinion as to whether or not they are subject to proprietary rights.

While the advice and information in this book are believed to be true and accurate at the date of publication, neither the authors nor the editors nor the publisher can accept any legal responsibility for any errors or omissions that may be made. The publisher makes no warranty, express or implied, with respect to the material contained herein.

Cover image designed by Freepik

Managing Director: Welmoed Spahr
Editorial Director: Todd Green
Acquisitions Editor: Natalie Pao
Development Editor: James Markham
Technical Reviewer: Logan West
Coordinating Editor: Jessica Vakili
Copy Editor: Teresa Horton
Compositor: SPi Global
Indexer: SPi Global
Artist: SPi Global

Distributed to the book trade worldwide by Springer Science+Business Media New York, 233 Spring Street, 6th Floor, New York, NY 10013. Phone 1-800-SPRINGER, fax (201) 348-4505, e-mail orders-ny@springer-sbm.com, or visit www.springeronline.com. Apress Media, LLC is a California LLC and the sole member (owner) is Springer Science + Business Media Finance Inc (SSBM Finance Inc). SSBM Finance Inc is a **Delaware** corporation.

For information on translations, please e-mail rights@apress.com, or visit http://www.apress.com/rights-permissions.

Apress titles may be purchased in bulk for academic, corporate, or promotional use. eBook versions and licenses are also available for most titles. For more information, reference our Print and eBook Bulk Sales web page at http://www.apress.com/bulk-sales.

Any source code or other supplementary material referenced by the author in this book is available to readers on GitHub via the book's product page, located at www.apress.com/978-1-4842-2892-0. For more detailed information, please visit http://www.apress.com/source-code.

Printed on acid-free paper

Contents at a Glance

Contents

About the Author

Jennifer Harder has worked in the graphic design industry for more than ten years. She has a degree in graphic communications and is currently teaching Acrobat, InDesign, and Dreamweaver courses at Langara College. As a freelancer, Jennifer frequently works with Adobe PDFs and checks them before they go to print or are uploaded to the Web. She enjoys talking about Adobe Software and her interests include writing, illustration, and working on her web sites.

Acknowledgments

For their patience and advice, I would like to thank the following people, without whom I could never have written this book. My parents encouraged me to read large computer textbooks that would one day inspire me to write my own books. My Dad reviewed the first draft before I sent a proposal. My program coordinator, Raymond Chow at Langara College, gave me the chance to teach evening courses when others would not give me that opportunity or believe that I had anything worthy to contribute. My printing boss, Eddie, at Pender Copy, Ltd., inspired and encouraged me to write this book that he thought every graphic designer should read. At Apress, I would like to thank Natalie and Jessica for showing me how to lay out a professional textbook and pointing out even when you think you've written it all there's still more to write. Thanks also go to Jim Markham and the technical reviewer Logan West for taking the time to test my files and their encouraging comments. Thank you also to the rest of the Apress team for printing this book and making my dream a reality. I am truly grateful and blessed.

Introduction

Welcome to the first step in an exciting journey I've called *Data Merge and Styles for Adobe InDesign CC 2018*. In the seven chapters that follow, you will discover that you can harness the power of Adobe InDesign's Data Merge and Style panels. Whether you're creating custom mailings or working on other mail-merge needs, you can familiarize yourself with this powerful InDesign panel in this in-depth, step-by-step guide. This book shows you how to easily create, edit, and print data merged documents that match specific branding and style guidelines.

You'll learn how to use Microsoft Excel to create a faster workflow and quickly turn your Adobe InDesign CC 2018 files into printer-ready files. In this book, we'll also look at how to apply paragraph and character styles to your text and how you can alter formatting using Global Regular Expressions Print (GREPs).

With *Data Merge and Styles for Adobe InDesign CC 2018* as your guide, you'll learn how to save time and money by mastering all the peculiarities and powerful features of Adobe InDesign Data Merge. By the end of this book, you'll be able to streamline your workflow and avoid using Microsoft Word's mail merge and back-and-forth edits.

What You'll Learn

- Chapter 1: Build a custom workspace for all your Data Merge projects.

- Chapter 2: Build a numbering sequence for tickets using paragraph styles.

- Chapter 3: Create single-record data merges for single-page and multipage documents that include paragraph styles.

- Chapter 4: Create single-record data merges with, text, images, and QR codes that includes paragraph styles.

- Chapter 5: Build a double numbering sequence for tickets and information cards with multiple Data Merge records.

- Chapter 6: Work with GREPs in conjunction with character and paragraph styles to customize data.

- Chapter 7: Learn some troubleshooting tips and test your knowledge with a quiz.

- At the end of each chapter you will create a print-ready PDF file using different workflow methods. These PDF documents can be either printed on your home or office printer or sent to your local print house.

Whether you're a student, a graphic designer, or a corporate administrator who needs to create documents for events, this is a valuable resource to have in your library of knowledge.

CHAPTER 1

■ ■ ■

Introduction: Creating a Workspace

Welcome to working with Data Merge and Styles in Adobe InDesign.

In 2005 when I started working with a print house as a freelance graphic artist, some of the clients that the owner of the print house and I worked for had to print various mailings for communication and corporate events. In the past, I had created labels for our clients using Microsoft Excel and Microsoft Word Mail Merge. However, there were instances where I had to lay out some of the artwork in Adobe InDesign or the client supplied only a PDF of the artwork. Working with these graphics in Microsoft Word along with a Mail Merge did not always produce the desired results. Often, I only had few hours to create the custom file that consisted of more than 100 pages. There was little time to experiment with a new layout in Word and setup of the Excel data when it was formatted incorrectly. I took some time, therefore, to learn the features of InDesign Data Merge and found that it was very much like the Mail Merge in Word. Over the years, my printing boss and I have had many clients ask us to create data merged files for their mailings and corporate events. The following chapters detail some of the main uses for Data Merge, but I am sure that after you have read this book you will be able to find additional ways to use the Data Merge within your company.

■ **Note** There are no Assignment files for this chapter.

Table 1-1 is an example of two custom cover letters where data from the Microsoft Excel file was either added via a Mail Merge in Microsoft Word or via the Data Merge Panel in Adobe InDesign. The data from the Excel file is shown in bold and italics for comparison purposes.

© Jennifer Harder 2017
J. Harder, *Data Merge and Styles for Adobe InDesign CC 2018*,
https://doi.org/10.1007/978-1-4842-3159-3_1

Table 1-1. *Data Merge Example of a Letter*

Letter 1	Letter 2
0001 John Smith 123 Any Street Toronto, ON V1R 2Q5 Dear **John**, Welcome to the sales convention, in your presentation package you will find	*0002 Mary Lewis 425 Broadview Ave Vancouver, BC V3Q 9R7* Dear **Mary**, Welcome to the sales convention, in your presentation package you will find ....

If you are new to Adobe InDesign CC, I would recommend that you read *Adobe InDesign CC Classroom in a Book* by Kelly Kordes Anton and John Cruise. Please note that although this book can teach you the basics of Adobe InDesign and some layout styles, it does not address Data Merge in any detail.

Note that this book does not address the creation of electronic publications (ePUB) in InDesign CC, although you could use the Data Merge feature in the process of a layout for a custom book or file, as you will see in later chapters. You will also be reviewing many of the options of the Paragraph and Character Styles panels as they relate to the Data Merge. However, those options that do not relate to the Data Merge or specifically to ePUB creation will be skipped over.

If you have used InDesign for several years and want to learn how to use the Data Merge panel efficiently for your next printing project, then I am sure that you will find this book to be very helpful.

As a review, let's begin by setting up the Adobe InDesign CC 2018 program and our workspace.

■ **Note** Adobe InDesign's Data Merge has been included in the program since version CS2. Although you might be able to complete most of the tutorials within this book with an older version of InDesign, the screen shots that you view might be different than what you see in your program. I recommend that you update to the latest version of InDesign CC with your Creative Cloud subscription.

For more information on Adobe software, visit `https://www.adobe.com/creativecloud/plans.html`.

Cleaning Up Your Workspace: Open Adobe InDesign CC 2018

If you use Adobe InDesign every day like I do, your interface might have become a bit cluttered. Let's start by cleaning it up. Refer to Figure 1-1.

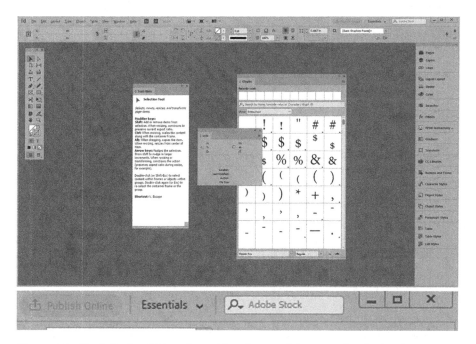

Figure 1-1. *The InDesign CC interface with a closeup of the menu for altering the workspace. Currently it is set to Essentials.*

In the upper right corner of the InDesign interface you will find the Workspaces as in Figures 1-1 and 1-2. Alternativelty, from the menu, you can go to Window ➤ Workspaces. Currently I am using the Essentials workspace, but you might be using a different one.

For this lesson, let's begin by resetting the workspace. From the Essentials drop-down menu, select Reset Essentials, as shown in Figure 1-2.

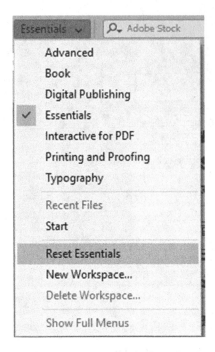

Figure 1-2. *The Essentials drop-down menu has Reset Essentials selected*

As displayed in Figure 1-3, the workspace is now considerably cleaner.

Figure 1-3. *The InDesign workspace is now cleaned up and ready for your next project*

> ■ **Note** If you select other workspaces, none of the workspaces contain the Data Merge panel. You will create a new workspace for that shortly so that you can use it for all the chapters in this book.

Create a New Document

From the File menu, choose New ➤ Document, as shown in Figure 1-4.

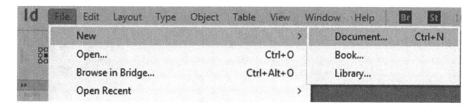

Figure 1-4. *Use the File menu to create a new document*

InDesign has a new panel so that you can easily choose to create a custom layout for print, web, or mobile or one of the document presets within the software. It also allows you to buy or use free templates others have created, as shown in Figure 1-5.

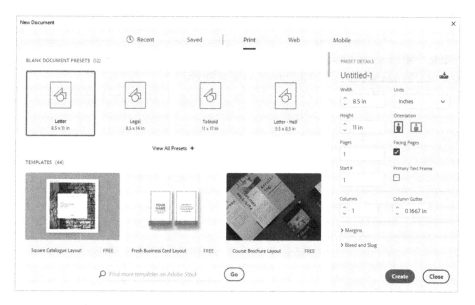

Figure 1-5. *The New Document dialog box with its assorted options*

For this book, you will focus on the Print tab and a new blank letter document.

Clear the Facing Pages check box, as you will be mostly working with a single-sheet layout.

Click Create, and a new document will appear as displayed in Figure 1-6.

Figure 1-6. *A new document appears in the InDesign interface ready for you to work with*

■ **Note**   If, for some reason, you clicked Save Document Preset while naming your document by mistake and saved the preset, refer to Figure 1-7.

Figure 1-7. Clicking Save Document Preset causes this message to appear. If you don't want to save this, click Cancel before continuing

You can remove the preset. Close the New Document dialog box and then under File ➤ Document Preset ➤ Define, click Delete and click OK to remove it. Click OK again to exit the dialog box. Refer to Figures 1-8 and 1-9.

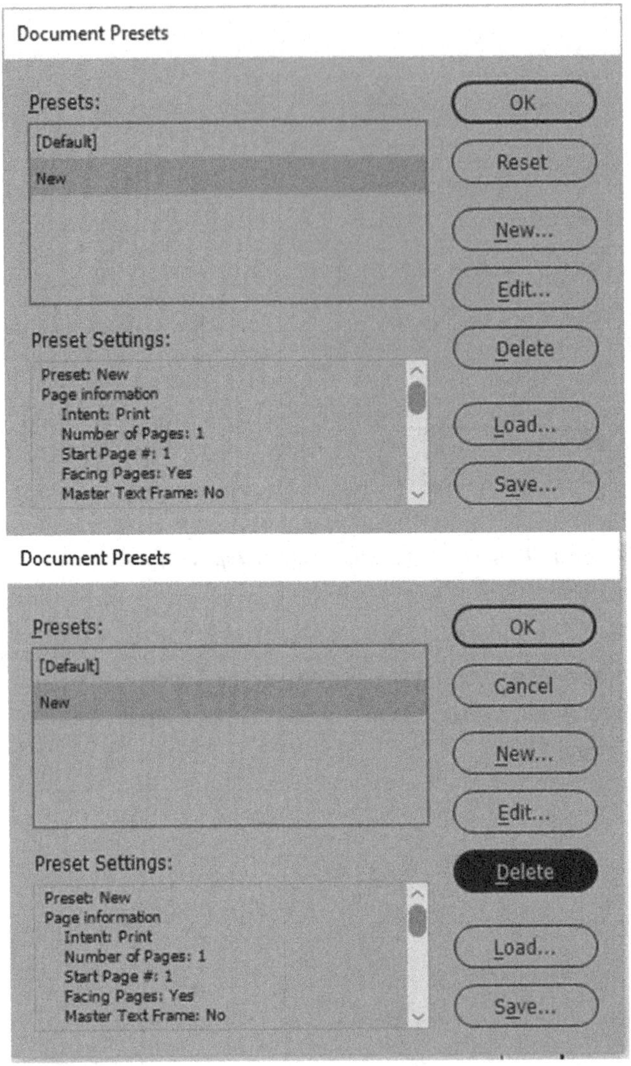

Document Presets

Presets:

[Default]
New

OK
Reset
New...
Edit...
Delete

Preset Settings:

Preset: New
Page information
    Intent: Print
    Number of Pages: 1
    Start Page #: 1
    Facing Pages: Yes
    Master Text Frame: No

Load...
Save...

Document Presets

Presets:

[Default]
New

OK
Cancel
New...
Edit...
Delete

Preset Settings:

Preset: New
Page information
    Intent: Print
    Number of Pages: 1
    Start Page #: 1
    Facing Pages: Yes
    Master Text Frame: No

Load...
Save...

Figure 1-8. *To remove unwanted document presets, click Delete*

Adobe InDesign

OK to delete the selected preset?

OK   Cancel

Figure 1-9. *Warning dialog box that results when removing a preset*

Optional: Removing Custom Page Sizes

Likewise, you might have custom page sizes that you want to remove so that they don't appear in the New Document Setting dialog box.

Go to File ➤ Document Setup to open the dialog box shown in Figure 1-10.

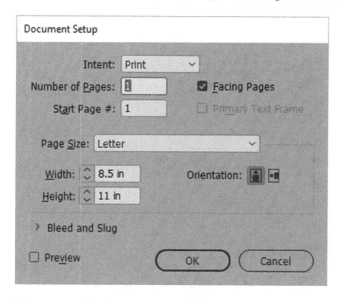

Figure 1-10. *The Document Setup dialog box*

As shown in Figure 1-11, from the Page Size drop-down menu, select Custom ....

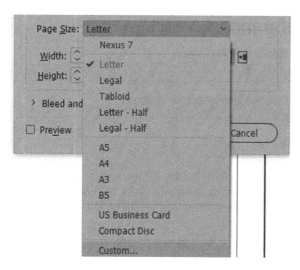

Figure 1-11. *From Document Setup dialog box Page Size drop-down menu, click Custom ....*

In this case I have one custom page size that I don't require anymore. You might have none, want to keep the ones you have, or create new ones, so this step is optional. Select the custom page size, click Delete, and then click OK to close the Custom Page Size dialog box (see Figure 1-12).

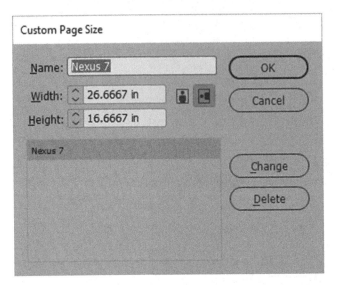

Figure 1-12. *Remove a custom page size by selecting it and clicking Delete*

Now let's adjust our preferences.

Setting Up Your Preferences

From the Main Menu go to Edit ➤ Preferences ➤ General.

___

■ **Note**   You will only be adjusting specific preferences for this book.

___

General Tab

On the General tab, make sure that the Show "Start" Workspace When No Documents Are Open check box is cleared. Because you want to open the new dialog box only when you decide to create a new file. Otherwise, leave the other settings as shown in Figure 1-13.

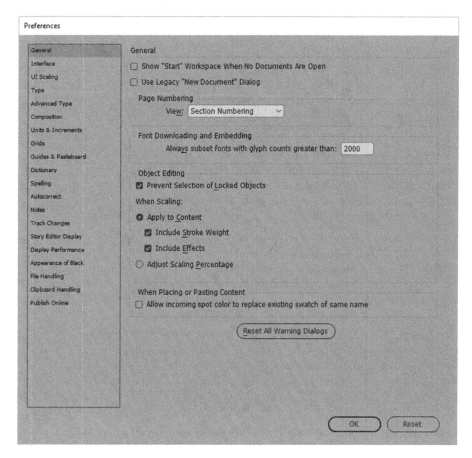

Figure 1-13. *Reviewing the General tab in the Preferences dialog box*

Interface Tab

Now click the Interface tab, which allows you to alter the color of an InDesign layout. Because I work in a printing environment, I prefer a neutral gray so that I can view colors as true as possible to print. A layout of black or white can strain the eyes and affect how you interpret color. You can also choose to have the pasteboard match the theme color. I usually leave the other settings at their defaults, but you can adjust how your cursors and gesture options react for tool tips. Panels settings affect how the panels will float, open, and display. Options also adjust display performance for graphics. Refer to Figure 1-14.

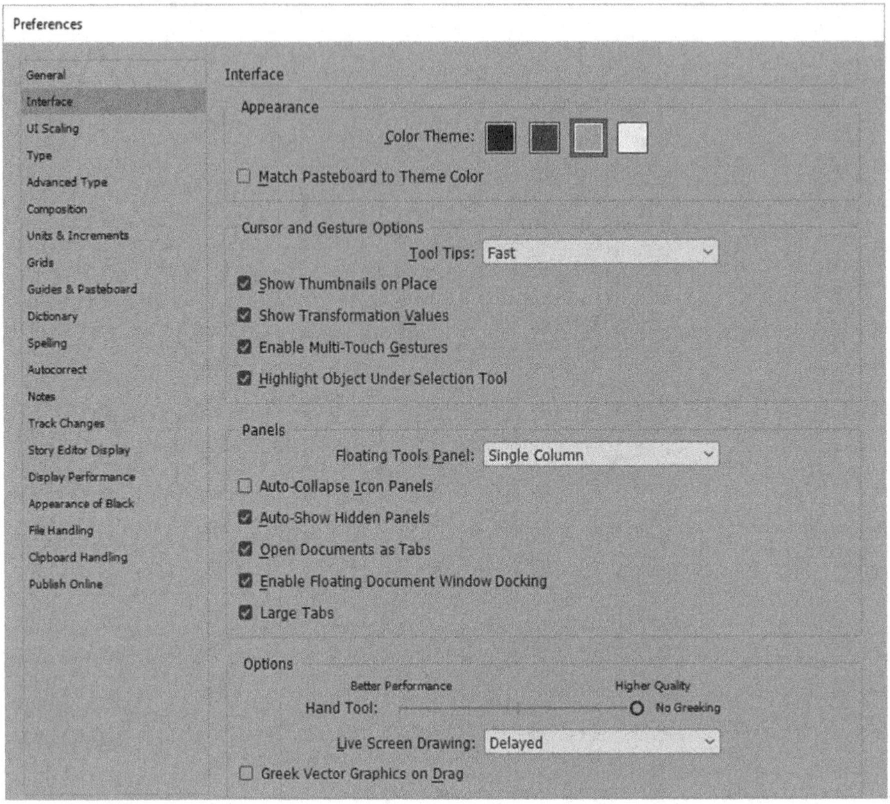

Figure 1-14. *The Interface tab in the Preferences dialog box*

You can leave the following tabs set at the program defaults:

- UI Scaling: User Interface Display

- Type: Type Options, Drag and Drop Editing, Smart Text Reflow

- Advanced Type: Character Setting, Input Method Options, Missing Glyph Protection, Default Composer, Type Contextual Controls

- Composition: Highlight and Text Wrap

Units & Increments Tab

Click the Units & Increments tab. For my Ruler Units Horizontal and Vertical settings, I will be using inches. If you prefer to use points and picas or some other unit of measurement, feel free to set this later. Otherwise leave the settings at the default, as shown in Figure 1-15.

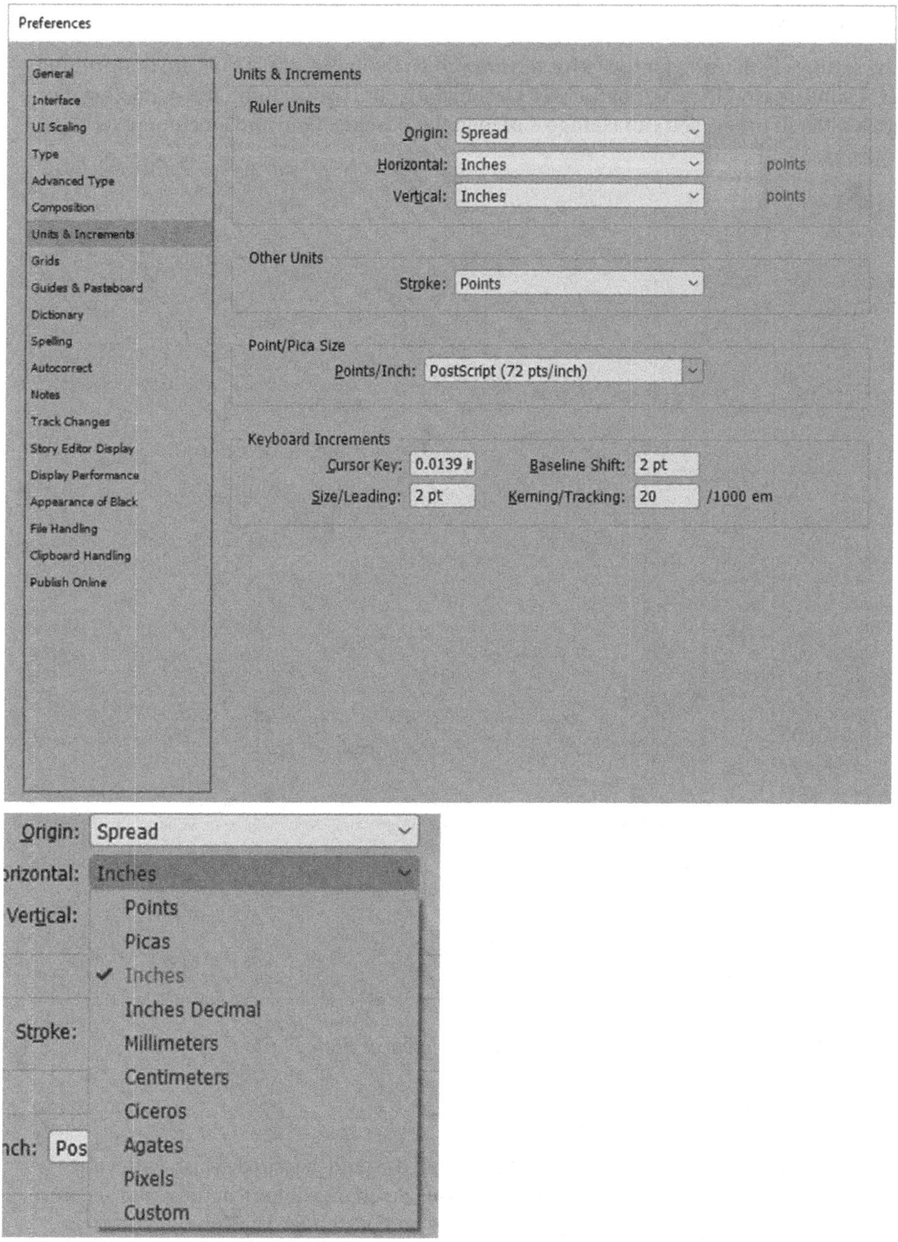

Figure 1-15. *Reviewing the Units & Increments tab of the Preferences dialog box*

Grids Tab

The settings I am using for the Grids tab are shown in Figure 1-16. Grids are nonprinting. If for some reason the color of the grid clashes with your artwork on screen, making the grids difficult to see, you can change it here in the Baseline Grid and Document Grid sections.

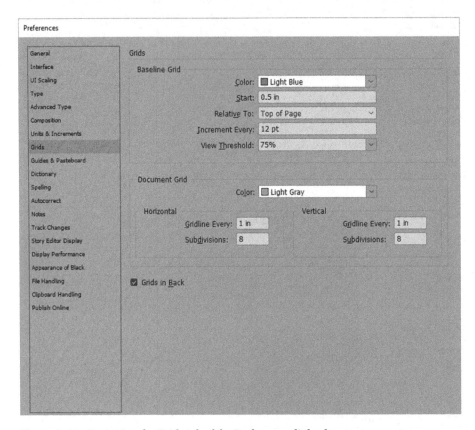

Figure 1-16. *Reviewing the Grids tab of the Preferences dialog box*

Guides & Pasteboard Tab

I left my setting at the default, but like the grids, if the guides visually clash with your artwork on screen, making it difficult to see, you can change it here in the Color section. You can also adjust various smart guide settings and pasteboard options, as shown in Figure 1-17.

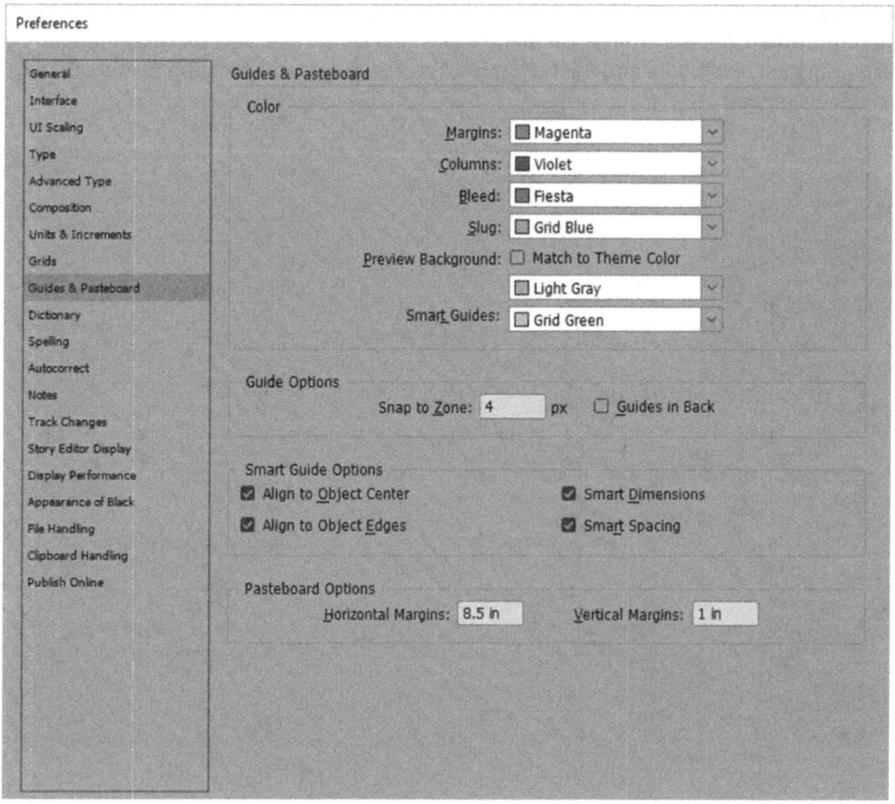

Figure 1-17. *Reviewing the Guides & Pasteboard tab of the Preferences dialog box*

Let's skip over a few more tabs and leave them at the default settings:

- Dictionary: Language, Hyphenation, User Dictionary
- Spelling: Find and Dynamic Spelling
- Autocorrect: Options and Language
- Notes: Assorted Options for the Notes tool
- Track Changes: Show, Change Bars
- Story Editor Display: Text display and cursor options

Display Performance Tab

Display performance relates to how graphics display in an InDesign file while you are working on the document. Leave these settings at the default of Typical (see Figure 1-18) so that you can see the graphic but it does not show in high resolution, using up a lot of processing power. If you need to preview a specific graphic, right-click it and select High-Quality display from the drop-down menu shown in Figure 1-19. Only that graphic will display in high resolution, and not the others. You will look at this function in more detail in later chapters.

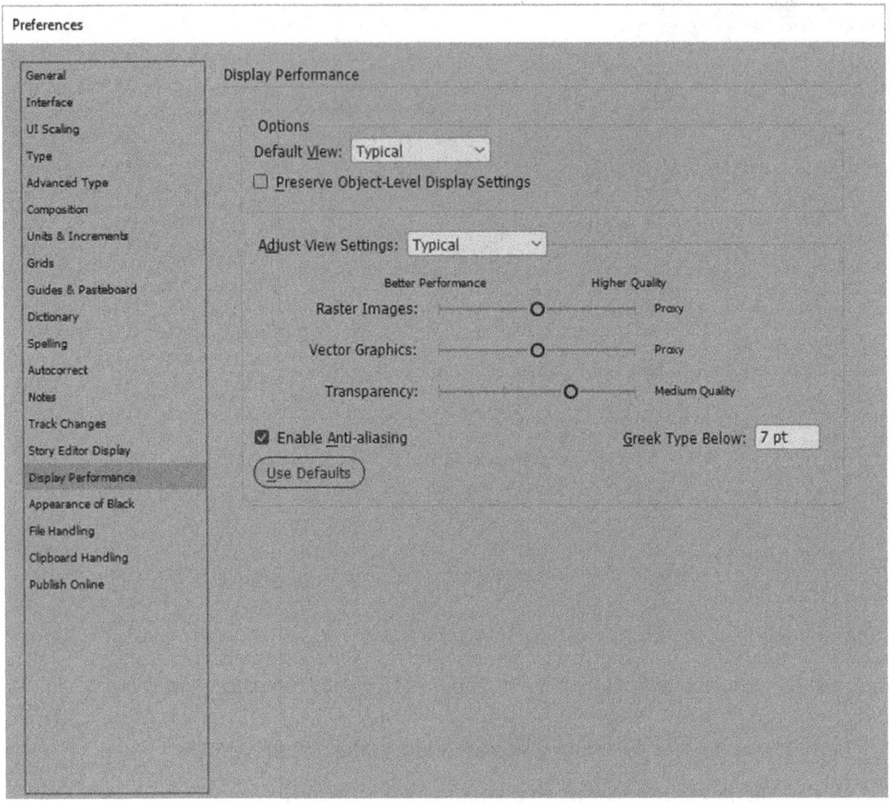

Figure 1-18. Reviewing the Display Performance tab of the Preferences dialog box

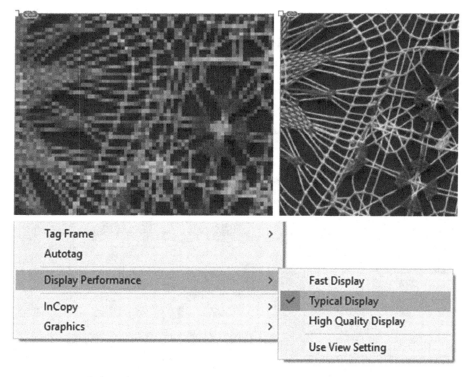

Figure 1-19. Adjusting display performance for specific images outside of the Preferences area

Appearance of Black Tab

Because you will be working in a printing environment, it is important to make sure that your blacks display accurately. Set the On Screen and Printing/Exporting options to Display All Blacks Accurately and Output All Blacks Accurately, respectively (see Figure 1-20). Rich Black is made up of 100% cyan, 100% magenta, 100% yellow, and 100% black.

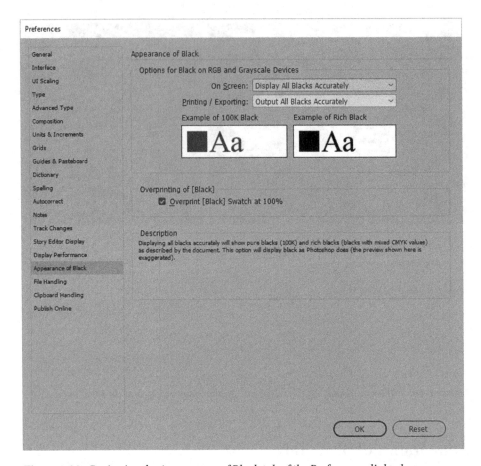

Figure 1-20. *Reviewing the Appearance of Black tab of the Preferences dialog box*

Black is simply 100% black, so its overall color appears duller. On screen when previewing the file, it is important to be aware of the difference, otherwise you might get unexpected results when the file goes to print.

Skip over the final three tabs:

- File Handling: Document Recovery Data, Saving InDesign Files, Snippet Import, Links

- Clipboard Handling: Clipboard and Pasting options

- Publish Online: Leave this setting cleared

When done, click OK to exit the Preferences dialog box and save your changes.

■ **Note**   If your preferences become corrupted or you need to set them to the defaults, according to Adobe Help make sure to do the following:

For Windows, start InDesign, and then press Shift+Ctrl+Alt. Click Yes when asked if you want to delete preference files.

For Mac OS, while pressing Shift+Option+Command+Control, start InDesign. Click Yes when asked if you want to delete preference files.

Continue Setting Up the Workspace

So far, you have been using the InDesign Menu bar to adjust your program settings. You will now begin to set up a workspace that you will use for the next chapters in this book on the topic of Data Merge.

Currently, your interface will look something like Figure 1-21 if you have chosen the Essentials workspace as your starting point.

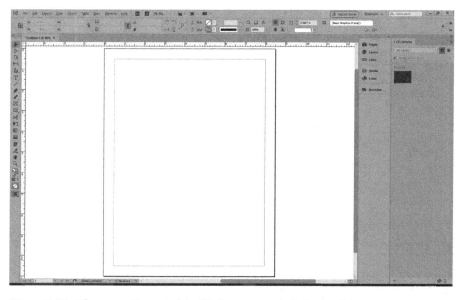

Figure 1-21. *The current layout of the Workspace area in InDesign CC*

Begin by adjusting the workspace, first removing and then adding various panels to the left and right that you will be using throughout the book.

From the Menu bar, go to the Window drop-down menu shown in Figure 1-22. There you will find a list of all the panels that can display in InDesign. For this book, I talk about specific ones that you will use for Data Merge.

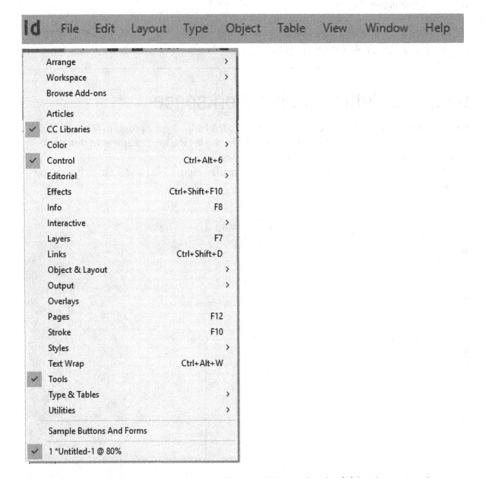

Figure 1-22. *The Window menu shows all available panels. The (>) leads you to other panels that are grouped under that menu name*

When a panel is open on the screen, it will be marked with a check mark. When not open, it not be checked. Select and clear the CC Libraries setting. Window ➤ CC Libraries is now removed from the display, as you will not be using this panel. Refer to Figure 1-23.

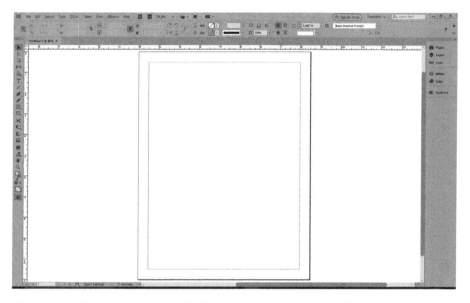

Figure 1-23. *The current layout of the Workspace area in InDesign CC with the CC Libraries removed*

You will see the Tools panel, shown in Figure 1-24, on the left side of the screen.

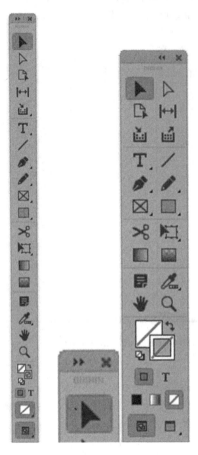

Figure 1-24. *The Tools panel in single- and double-column settings. Clicking the small arrows on the handle adjusts its size and layout.*

With your mouse, click the upper handle and drag it to the right side so it becomes undocked and floats over the pasteboard. Click the small upper arrows in the tool to expand the tool to two rows, which makes the color selection easier to adjust for fill and stroke. Note that if it displays horizontally, you might have to click the arrows again to toggle through the layout options. The screen should look something like Figure 1-25.

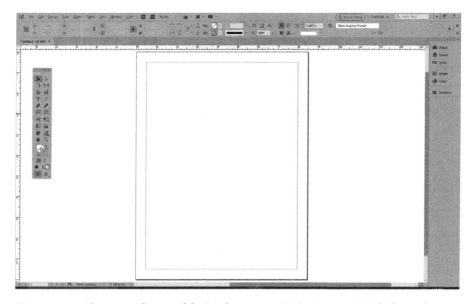

Figure 1-25. *The current layout of the Workspace area in InDesign CC with the Tools panel undocked*

Figures 1-26 and 1-27 provide a breakdown of the tools within the Tools panel.

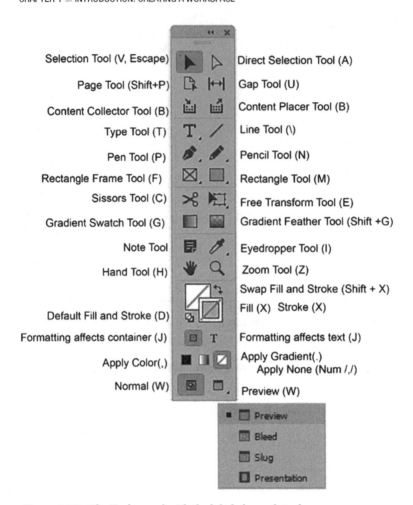

Figure 1-26. *The Tools panel with the labels for each tool*

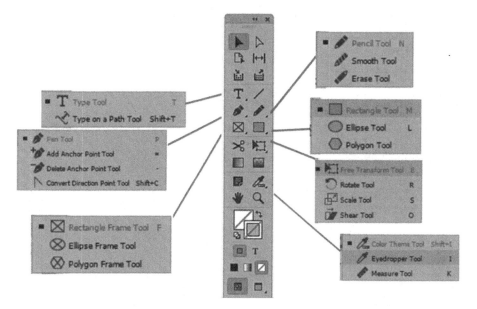

Figure 1-27. *The Tools panel with the labels for each tool in the pull-out menus*

■ **Note** If you need details about what each tool is used for, go to Window ➤ Utilities ➤ Tool Hints. As you select each tool, a different message will display, explaining what each tool is for. Refer to Figure 1-28.

25

Figure 1-28. The Tool Hints panel

Controls Panel

On the top of the interface, you will find the Controls panel. From here you can control such things as color, alignment, and stroke on various text and objects. Sometimes it is easier to work in this panel than using the various separate panels I discuss shortly. The appearance of this panel changes based on what tool is currently being used, As shown in Figure 1-29.

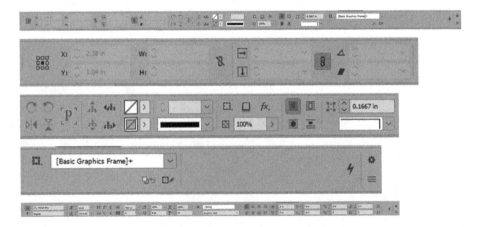

Figure 1-29. The Controls panel and a close-up view of some of the available options

Currently docked on the right side, clicking each one will display the actual panel. By clicking another panel or the Panel tab you can display the settings for that panel.

Pages Panel

The Pages panel displays a thumbnail of that page and the master page template. If you clear the Display Facing Pages check box, you will have a slightly different layout in the master page area, as shown in Figure 1-30.

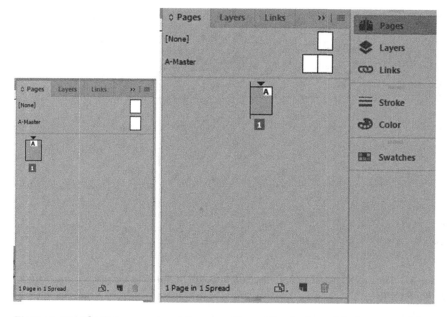

Figure 1-30. The Pages panel and its general layout for single and facing pages. Other menu options can be found in the panel's upper right drop-down menu.

Layers Panel

The Layers panel, shown in Figure 1-31, shows how many layers the document has, similar to this setting with Photoshop and Illustrator. Layers can be hidden by turning off the eye or locked and unlocked by clicking the square next to the eye. When a layer is editable it will have a pen on the layer. A locked layer is indicated by a strikethough on the pen icon. If there is an object or frame on the layer selected, the small square on that layer will be filled. Layers can have sublayers so that you can organize your artwork and drag it with your mouse up or down.

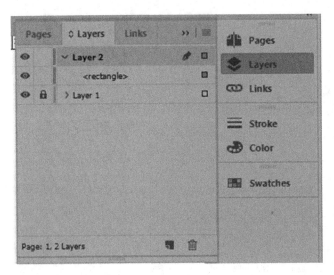

Figure 1-31. The Layers panel. Other menu options can be found in the panel's upper right drop-down menu

Links Panel

The Links panel, displayed in Figure 1-32, shows how many images are in the document, what pages they are on, and information about the images.

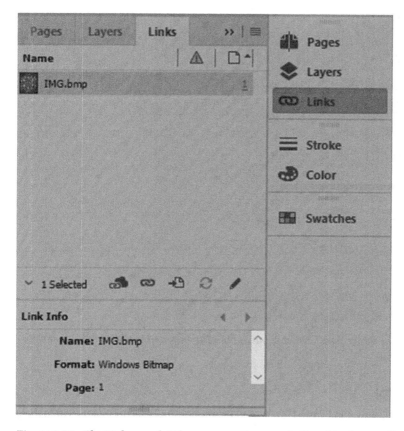

Figure 1-32. *The Links panel. Other menu options can be found in the panel's upper right drop-down menu*

The following panels can also be accessed through the Window menu, but they are already docked on the right side.

Stroke Panel

The Stroke panel, shown in Figure 1-33, includes settings for stroke (line thickness) or border frames of an image. Borders can have different weights, colors, gradients, and effects applied to them.

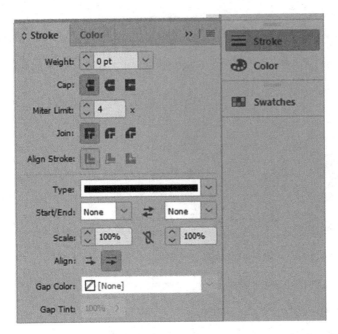

Figure 1-33. *The Stroke panel. Other menu options can be found in the panel's upper right drop-down menu.*

Color Panel

The Color panel, shown in Figure 1-34, is used for altering and selecting colors within the document.

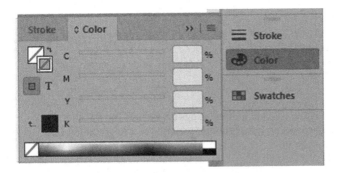

Figure 1-34. *The Color panel. Other menu options can be found in the panel's upper right drop-down menu.*

Swatches Panel

The Swatches panel, displayed in Figure 1-35, displays the current colors that are defaults or have been created or imported into the document. The Swatches area can also contain spot colors and various gradients.

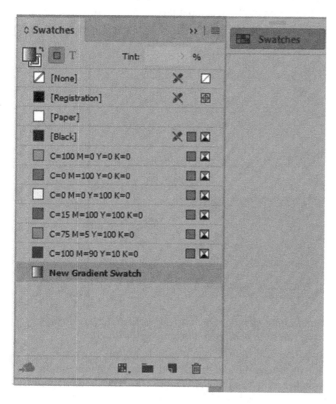

Figure 1-35. *The Swatches panel. Other menu options can be found in the panel's upper right drop-down menu.*

Now let's add the following panels to our dock station on the right.

Gradient Panel

To open the Gradient panel, go to Windows and open Color ➤ Gradient.

When it first appears, the Gradient panel will be floating on the screen, as shown in Figure 1-36.

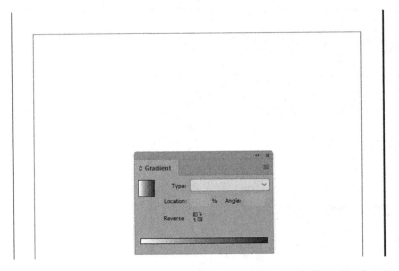

Figure 1-36. *The Gradient panel. Other menu options can be found in the panel's upper right drop-down menu. Here you can see it floating in the center of the interface*

With your mouse, grab the upper handle and drag it to the docking station on the right until it highlights the Swatches panel, as shown in Figure 1-37. The Gradient panel can be used to add gradients to fills and strokes of objects and text.

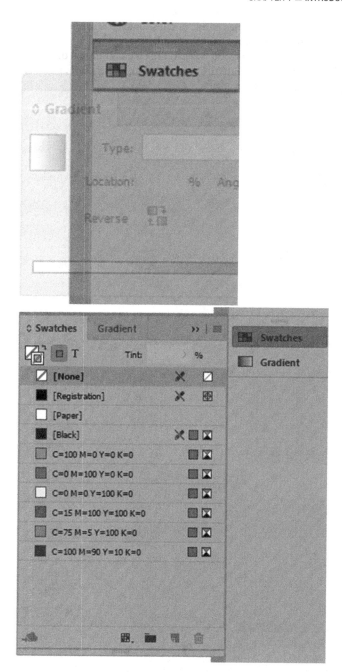

Figure 1-37. *The Gradient panel is now docked with the Swatches panel*

It should now be docked with it the Swatches panel, and it should look something like Figure 1-37. You can now adjust any gradient with the Gradient panel.

If you want to keep the panel docked separately you can drag it out and then drag it back in, making sure the highlight is underneath the Swatches panel, as shown in Figure 1-38. Now it is no longer part of a tabbed group.

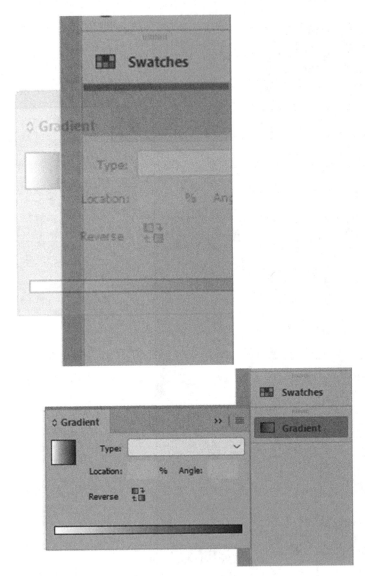

Figure 1-38. *The Gradient panel is still docked but separate from the Swatches panel*

Continue to dock more panels. Repeat the earlier docking steps and add the following panels. Open them so that they are on screen and then start docking them on the right.

Effects Panel

Use the Effects panel, shown in Figure 1-39, for transparency and drop shadows on your objects and frames. You can also use these same settings in the Objects Styles menu, as you will see in later chapters.

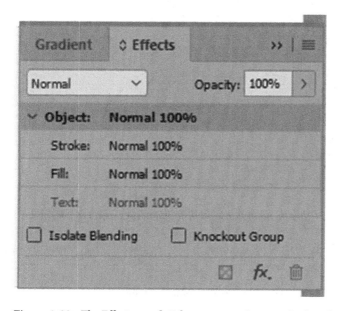

Figure 1-39. *The Effects panel. Other menu options can be found in the panel's upper right drop-down menu.*

Info Panel

Information on coordinates of the mouse and height and width of an object are displayed in the Info panel, shown in Figure 1-40.

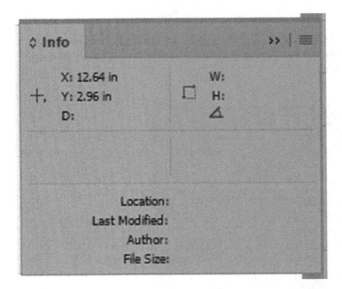

Figure 1-40. *The Info panel. Other menu options can be found in the panel's upper right drop-down menu*

Align Panel

The Align panel, shown in Figure 1-41, is used to align objects on the page.

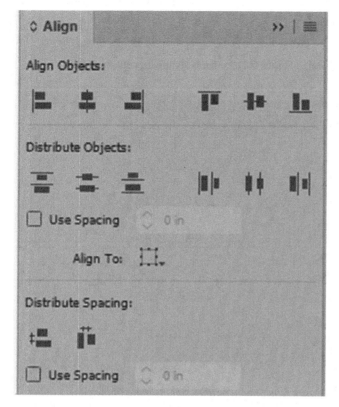

Figure 1-41. *The Align panel. Other menu options can be found in the panel's upper right drop-down menu.*

Styles
Cell Styles Panel

The Cell Styles panel, displayed in Figure 1-42, controls styling for cells in a table.

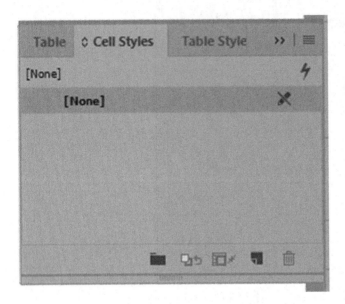

Figure 1-42. *The Cell Styles panel. Other menu options can be found in the panel's upper right drop-down menu.*

Character Styles Panel

Styling for letters or words within a sentence is determined in the Character Styles panel shown in Figure 1-43.

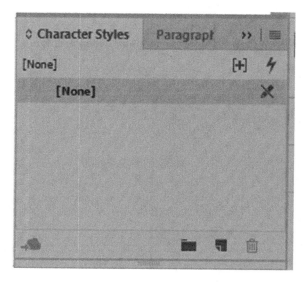

Figure 1-43. *The Character Styles panel. Other menu options can be found in the panel's upper right drop-down menu.*

Object Styles Panel

The Object Styles panel, displayed in Figure 1-44, controls styling for frames and borders of boxes.

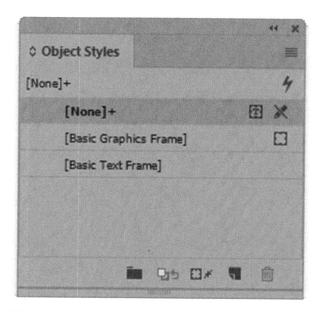

Figure 1-44. *The Object Styles panel. Other menu options can be found in the panel's upper right drop-down menu.*

Paragraph Styles Panel

The Paragraph Styles panel, shown in Figure 1-45, provides options for styling an entire paragraph.

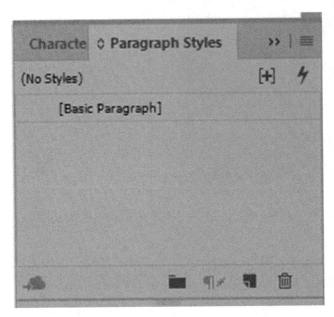

Figure 1-45. *The Paragraph Styles panel. Other menu options can be found in the panel's upper right drop-down menu.*

Table Styles Panel

The Table Styles panel, shown in Figure 1-46, controls styling for tables.

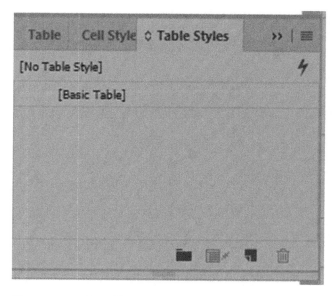

Figure 1-46. *The Table Styles panel. Other menu options can be found in the panel's upper right drop-down menu.*

Text Wrap Panel

The settings in the Text Wrap panel, shown in Figure 1-47, allow text to wrap around a framed object or graphic. Many of these options can also be found in the Object Styles Panel.

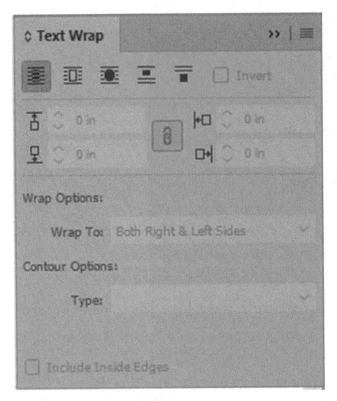

Figure 1-47. *The Text Wrap panel. Other menu options can be found in the panel's upper right drop-down menu.*

Types and Tables
Character Panel

The Character panel, shown in Figure 1-48, is used for working with text outside of character styles.

■ **Tip** Once you have designed a style using this tool, you can highlight the text and click the New Styles button in the Character Styles panel and it will be added to the list ready to be renamed.

Figure 1-48. *The Character panel. Other menu options can be found in the panel's upper right drop-down menu.*

Glyphs Panel

The Glyphs panel allows you to work with characters found within a specific font. Sometimes there are additional characters that you cannot easily locate using the keyboard, for example, Dingbats or Webdings font. This panel is shown in Figure 1-49.

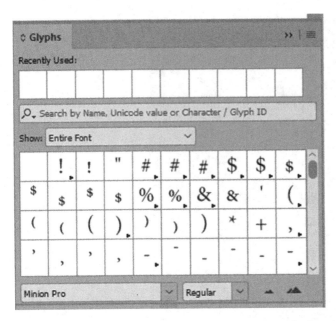

Figure 1-49. *The Glyphs panel. Other menu options can be found in the panel's upper right drop-down menu.*

Paragraph Panel

The Paragraph panel, shown in Figure 1-50, is used for working with a paragraph outside of styles.

■ **Tip**   Once you have designed a style using this tool in combination with the Character tool, you can highlight the text and click the New Styles button in the Paragraph Styles panel and it will be added to the list ready to be renamed.

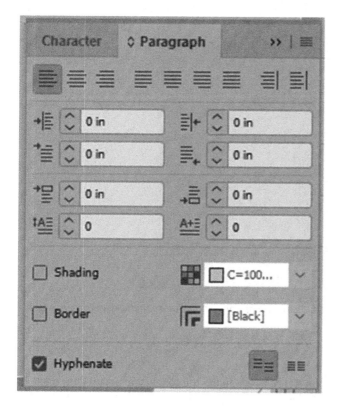

Figure 1-50. The Paragraph panel. Other menu options can be found in the panel's upper right drop-down menu.

Table Panel

The Table panel, displayed in Figure 1-51, is used for working with tables outside of styles.

■ **Tip** Once you have designed a style using this tool you can highlight the table and click the New Styles button in the Table Styles panel and it will be added to the list ready to be renamed and adjusted further with Cell styles.

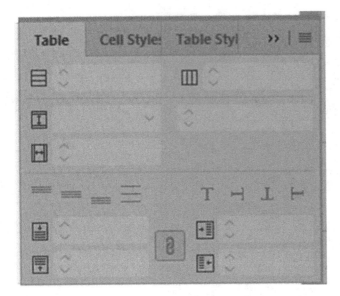

Figure 1-51. *The Table panel. Other menu options can be found in the panel's upper right drop-down menu.*

Data Merge Panel

The Data Merge panel, shown in Figure 1-52, handles the connection between the data source and InDesign. You will be looking at this tool in detail throughout Chapters 3 through 7.

Figure 1-52. *The Data Merge panel. Other menu options can be found in the panel's upper right drop-down menu.*

■ **Note** When you are selecting panels that come in a tabbed group with ones you don't want, drag them out by the tab and click the X in the top right corner of that panel to close the unwanted panel. Refer to Figure 1-53.

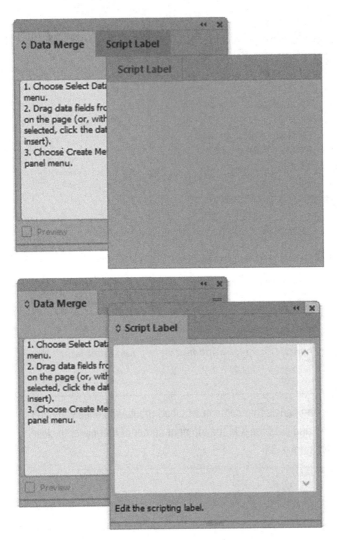

Figure 1-53. *When a panel like the Script Label panel appears and you don't want it to be part of the workspace, use the mouse to grab the tab and pull it away. You can then click the upper X in the panel to close it, leaving the panel you want to dock.*

Your interface docking on the right side should now look something like Figure 1-54.

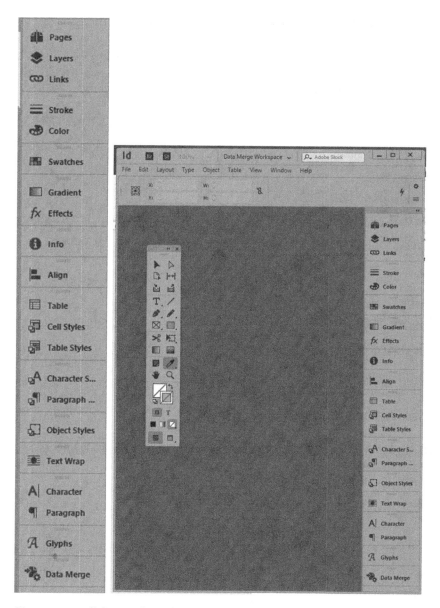

Figure 1-54. All the panels you have selected are now docked on the right

49

Now you will finish creating your new workspace. In the upper right corner, on the Essentials menu, click New Workspace, as shown in Figure 1-55.

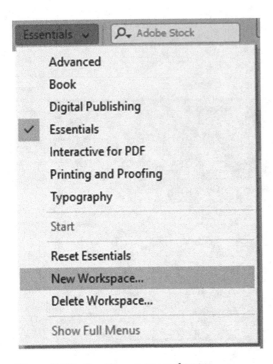

Figure 1-55. *Creating a new workspace*

In the New Workspace dialog box, change the name to Data Merge Workspace, as shown in Figure 1-56.

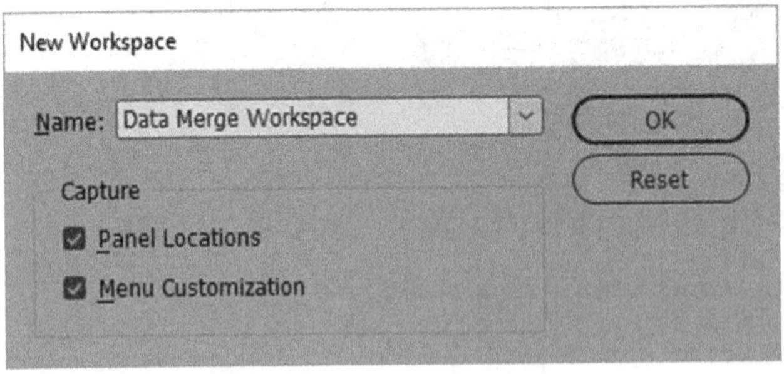

Figure 1-56. *The New Workspace dialog box*

Make sure that both options in the Capture section are selected so that if you drag panels out you can easily reset them back to their original location.

Click OK to confirm and close the dialog box. You have now added a new workspace to your list, as shown in Figure 1-57.

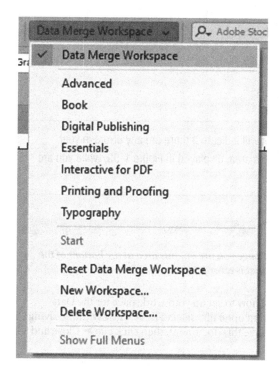

Figure 1-57. The new workspace is added to the top of the list

You can test it out by dragging the panels around and then selecting Reset Data Merge Workspace so that the panels will return to where they were placed for the next lesson.

If at some point you want to remove this workspace, click Delete Workspace and then create a new custom workspace to suit your needs. Do not select All, but only the one you want to delete, as shown in Figure 1-58.

Figure 1-58. *Deleting a custom workspace.*

■ **Note** The lower half of your document will indicate if there are any errors in your document. Make sure to keep an eye on this area, displayed in Figure 1-59, while you are working with the Data Merge.

Figure 1-59. *Along with telling you what page you are on, this area at the bottom of the interface indicates that the current document is error free*

This concludes the introduction and how to set up your workspace for the Data Merge. If you do not plan to save the current open file, select File ➤ Close without saving changes. Otherwise, click File ➤ Save to save this document, then click File ➤ Close and File ➤ Exit InDesign CC.

Summary

In this chapter, you reviewed how to clean up InDesign, adjust some preference settings, and create a custom Data Merge workspace that you will be using for the remainder of the book. Along the way you also did a quick review of the panels that you can use to complete Data Merge projects. Many of the panels are explored in further detail as you progress through the chapters. However, if there are any panels you are unsure about, make sure to review them in *Adobe InDesign CC Classroom in a Book,* mentioned earlier in the chapter.

CHAPTER 2

▦ ▦ ▦

Working with Paragraph Styles to Create Sequential Numbering

Project: Creating a Raffle Ticket Layout for Print

▦ **Note**   If you want to work along in this lesson or review the result, download your Chapter 2 files from http://www.apress.com/9781484231586. Work with the file with the label "Start." The file with the label "End" and the PDFs are the final result.

InDesign CC has several panels that you can use for styling text and images. For this chapter, you will be focusing on using the Paragraph Styles panel (see Figure 2-1) and its Bullets and Numbering tab to create sequential numbers for some raffle tickets. In addition, you will work with the Pages, Layer, and Align panels to complete your layout. Refer to Figure 2-2.

© Jennifer Harder 2017
J. Harder, *Data Merge and Styles for Adobe InDesign CC 2018*,
https://doi.org/10.1007/978-1-4842-3159-3_2

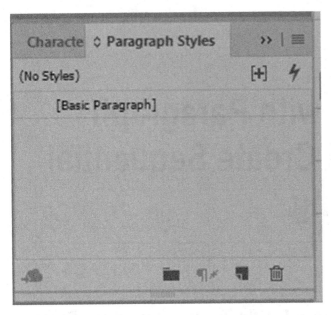

Figure 2-1. *The Paragraph Styles panel. When a new paragraph style is added you can double-click it to open the Paragraph Style Options dialog box and adjust settings for that style.*

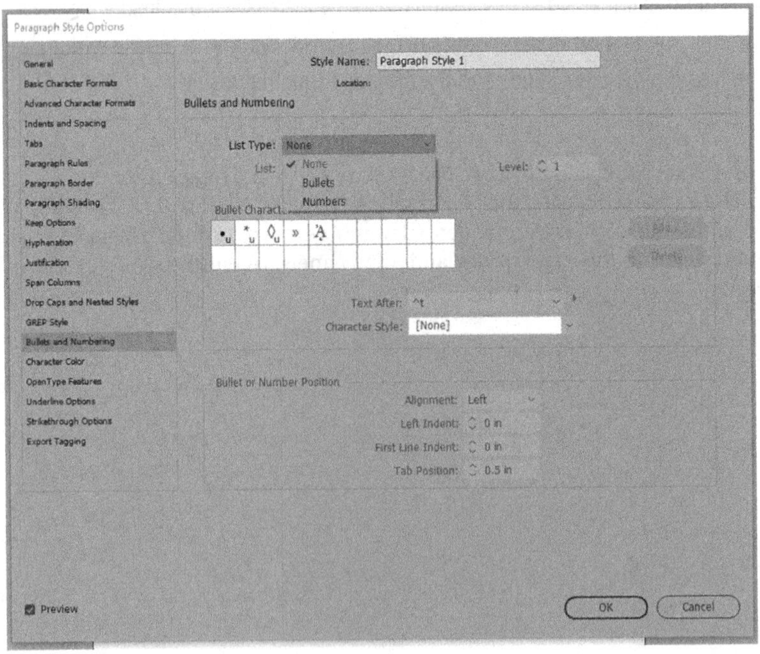

Figure 2-2. *The Paragraph Style Options dialog box Bullets and Numbering tab*

Working with Pages, Layers, and the Selection Tools

If you have created printing layouts before, you will remember that for small items like tickets you can have more than one item on a sheet. The amount on the sheet is referred to by the number and then "up." For example, three-up means three of the same items laid out on one sheet of paper, ten-up is ten items on one sheet, and so on. Each of the items is surrounded by crop marks evenly laid out around the item so that when the print contractor prints the item, they know where to cut (see Figure 2-3). This way each item is to the exact same size.

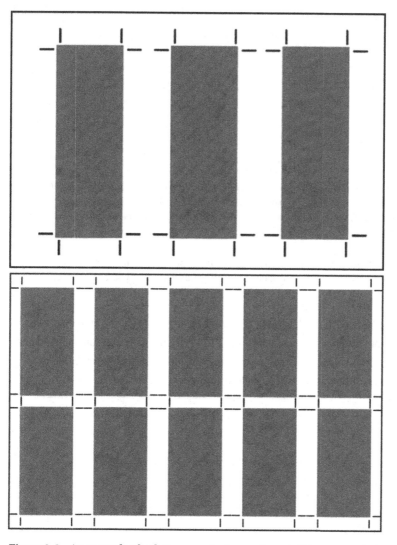

Figure 2-3. *An example of a three-up and a ten-up layout. The crop marks have been exaggerated here for viewing purposes.*

Sometimes some of the graphic will go beyond or into the crop mark area. This excess area is known as the *bleed*. When the card is cut out of the paper it makes it appear that the graphic runs from edge to edge of the card rather than leaving some white border around the card, as shown in the example in Figure 2-4.

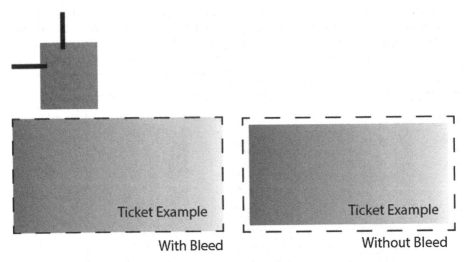

Figure 2-4. *If you want to have your design have the color run to the edge, you need to add bleed so that it slightly overlaps the crop marks. The dotted edge represents the cut item. If you don't add bleed, you will have a white edge, which might not be the effect you were trying to achieve.*

This tutorial assumes that you know something about crop mark layout; however, feel free to refer to my examples in the chapter folders as a guide if you are unsure.

■ **Note**   If you are working with a CMYK document make sure to set the crop marks you create to the color swatch of [Registration] (100 C 100 Y 100M 100K). You can do that under Window ➤ Color ➤ Swatches (F6). Using your Selection tool (V), select the crop marks stroke and select Registration from the list. Refer to Figure 2-5.

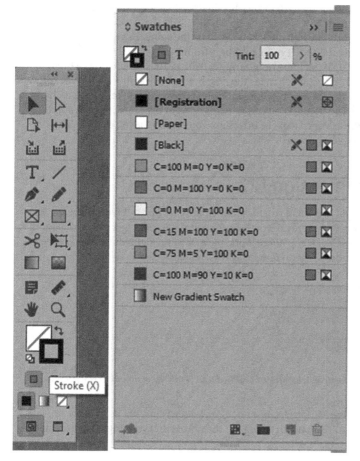

Figure 2-5. The Tools panel and Swatches panel are used to set the color of the crop marks to the color of [Registration]

Unless you are creating an all-black-and-white project, do not choose black, as this will only show the crop marks on the black plate. You need there to be a color on the other cyan, magenta, and yellow plates so that whether printing with an offset press or color laser printer you can see if the device is having any alignment issues and adjust the printer setting accordingly.

If you are creating your own custom layout, check with the print house you are working with to determine if they require you to add any additional printer marks to your page. For this lesson, you will assume that you are doing the printing in house on your color laser or inkjet printer.

Download the Chapter 2 zip folder from this link: ****. There you will find the files you need for this project.

Consistency is important when all tickets are to be the same. However, for raffle tickets you need custom numbers. Typing numbers from 1 to 100 might be easy, but what if you must type 1 to 1000? What if the numbering is 0001 to 1000, or includes a break like 1000 to 3000. What if the client changes the numbering style at the last minute? How could you type all these numbers without making errors? What if you only have an hour to work on the project? The point is you can't do this on your own on a short deadline. Don't panic; with a little advance work in InDesign, you can do the job quickly. The following sections show you how.

Open Adobe InDesign CC

To begin, open InDesign CC 2018. If you have not already set up your workspace, make sure to go back to Chapter 1 and review on the procedure for creating a workspace for the Data Merge. Otherwise select Data Merge Workspace or Reset Data Merge Workspace from the InDesign drop-down menu now, as shown in Figure 2-6.

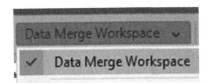

Figure 2-6. *Set or reset your workspace to Data Merge Workspace to begin the project*

If you were beginning the files from scratch, you would choose File ➤ New Document (see Figure 2-7) and begin laying out the tickets that you might have created in Photoshop or Illustrator.

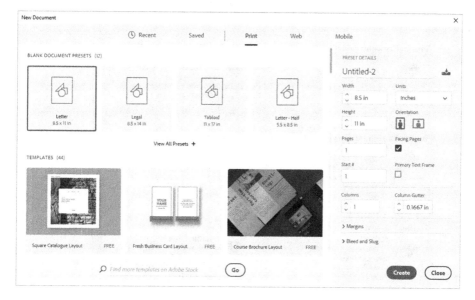

Figure 2-7. *You can set up the size of a new print product in the New Document dialog box*

However, for this chapter, choose File ➤ Open for the document (Raffle_10_up-Start.indd) in the Chapter 2 folder that contains the ticket design layout I have already created.

In my example, Figure 2-8 is a screen shot of my tickets that are ten-up on a sheet with crop marks. They are ready to have numbers added.

59

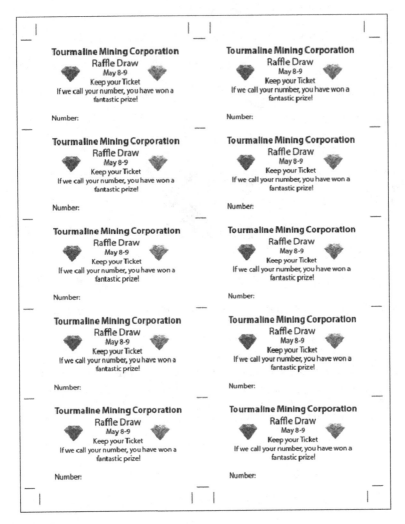

Figure 2-8. *Ten-up layout of raffle tickets*

The raffle tickets are 3.5 × 2 inches, business card size. A larger view of one of the tickets is displayed in Figure 2-9. I have left a space for my raffle number.

Figure 2-9. A close-up of a raffle ticket

■ **Note** The graphics and crop marks are on the Master Page A-Master and not on page one. I will explain why I did this later in the chapter. For now, stay on page one.

Working with the Layers

Go to Window ➤ Layers. The layout is nearly complete. It has two layers in the Layer panel, as shown in Figure 2-10. The CropMarks layer contains the printer's marks so that they will know where to cut the tickets later, and the Text layer contains the background image and text.

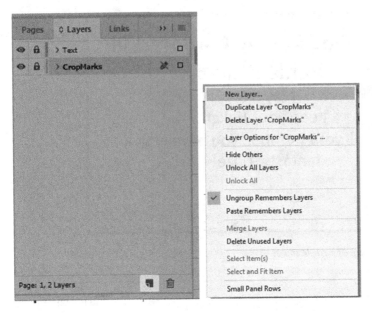

Figure 2-10. Currently the Layer panel has two layers. The New Layer button is located at the bottom of the panel to the left of the trash can icon. Alternately, you can choose New Layer from the menu in the upper right of the panel.

You will now create a new layer for the raffle numbers. Click Create New Layer at the bottom of the Layers panel and double-click it to rename or choose New Layer from the side menu option on the top right and open the Layer Options dialog box, shown in Figure 2-11.

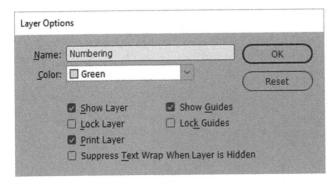

Figure 2-11. The Layer Options dialog box allows you to give the layer a name and set another layer color

Double-click the new layer and name it Numbering, as in Figure 2-11. Click OK to close the Layer Options dialog box. Keep the Text and CropMarks layers locked so you don't move an item by accident. Make sure to drag the Numbering layer to the top of the list if it is not already there, as shown in Figure 2-12, and leave it unlocked so you can edit it in the next step.

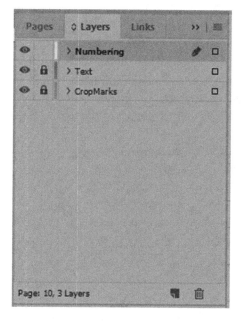

Figure 2-12. *The new layers has been added to the Layers panel and moved to the top of the list*

Working with the Selection Tool

On the new Numbering layer, with your mouse, draw and drag out a text box with the Type tool near the word Number: on the first ticket in the upper left; this will be the first raffle number. You can resize the box with the Selection Tool (V) if you think it is too large or too small (see Figure 2-13).

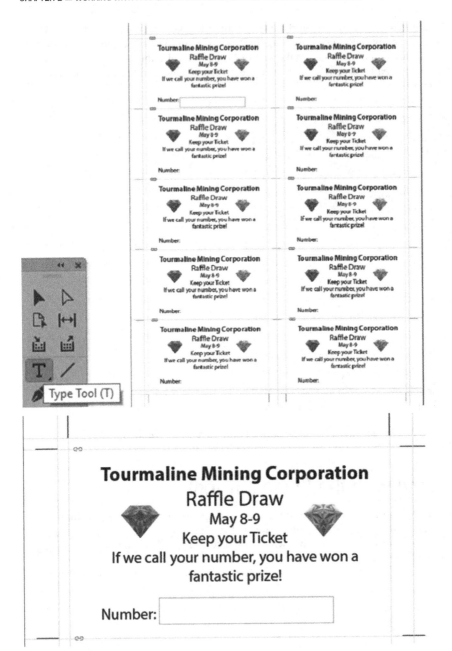

Figure 2-13. Use the Type tool to create a text box next to the Number: text on your first raffle ticket in the upper left of the page

Do not type into the text box yet. First, you will create the Numbering style using Paragraph Styles. Click somewhere on your pasteboard so that no text is selected.

Working with the Paragraph Styles Panel and Dialog Box

Click Window ➤ Styles ➤ Paragraph Styles. Create a new style by clicking the New Paragraph Style icon at the bottom right of the Paragraph Styles panel. Alternately you can choose New Paragraph Style from the upper right menu in the panel, as shown in Figure 2-14.

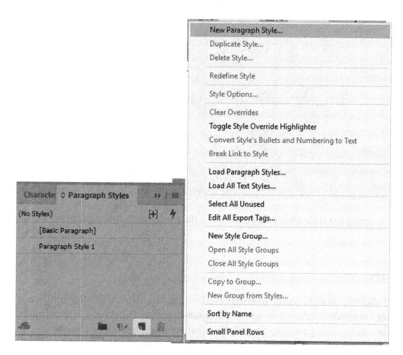

Figure 2-14. *To create a new paragraph style, either click the Create New Style button to the left of the trash can or select New Paragraph Style from the upper right menu*

Double-click Paragraph Style 1 and rename it Numbering Style on the General tab of the Paragraph Style Options dialog box as shown in Figure 2-15.

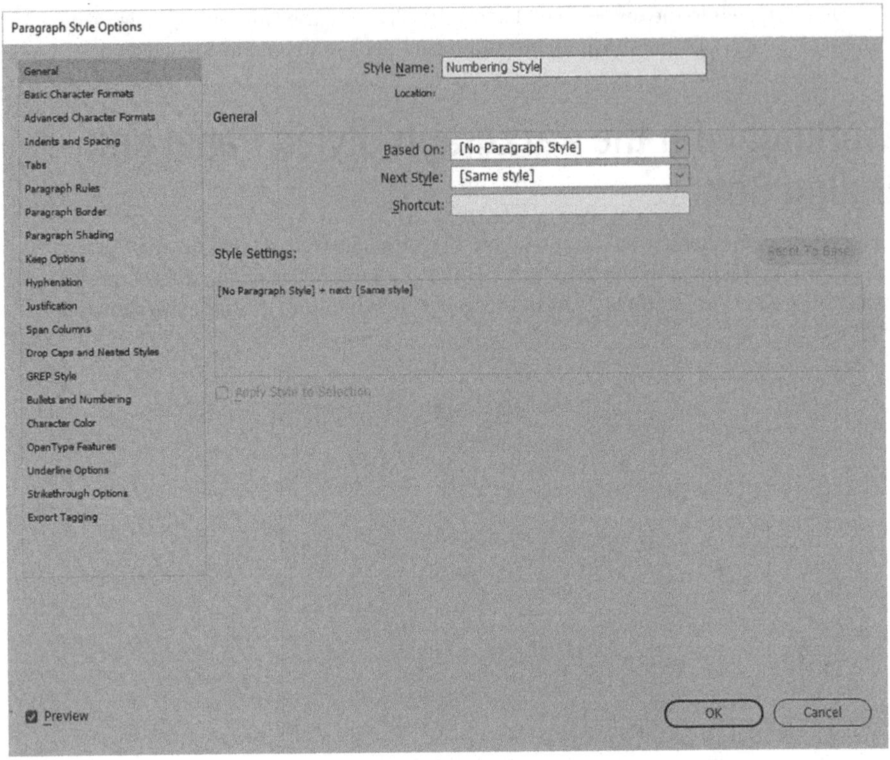

Figure 2-15. Renaming the style on the General tab of the Paragraph Style Options dialog box

General Tab

The General tab allows users to change the Style Name. You can also choose if the style is based on another currently used style from the drop-down menu. Otherwise, when you press the Enter key to create a paragraph break, the next style will be something else in the Paragraph Styles list. You can also add a keyboard shortcut to make it easier to apply options. The Style Settings box provides an overview of all the settings that have been applied collectively on other tabs within this dialog box. (This area might look slightly different depending on what styles you choose.) For now, leave the as Based On: setting set to [No Paragraph Style] and the Next Style setting set to [Same style].

Now move down to the Bullets and Numbering tab of the Paragraph Style Options dialog box.

Bullets and Numbering Tab

The Bullets and Numbering tab deals with list styles, levels, the formatting of the numbers and their positioning, and whether they are bullets or numbers. Refer to Figure 2-16.

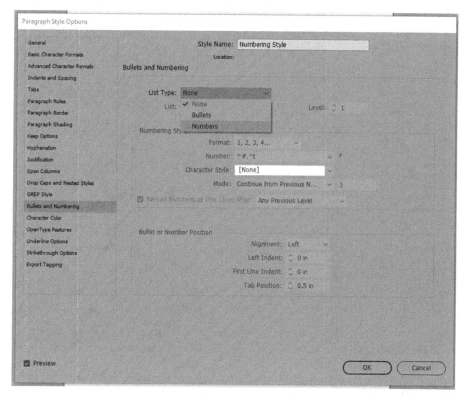

Figure 2-16. *The Bullets and Numbering tab of the Paragraph Style Options dialog box. Settings are defaulted to None until you choose Bullets or Numbers.*

You can see the default setting for numbering here. Let's make some changes, as shown in Figure 2-17.

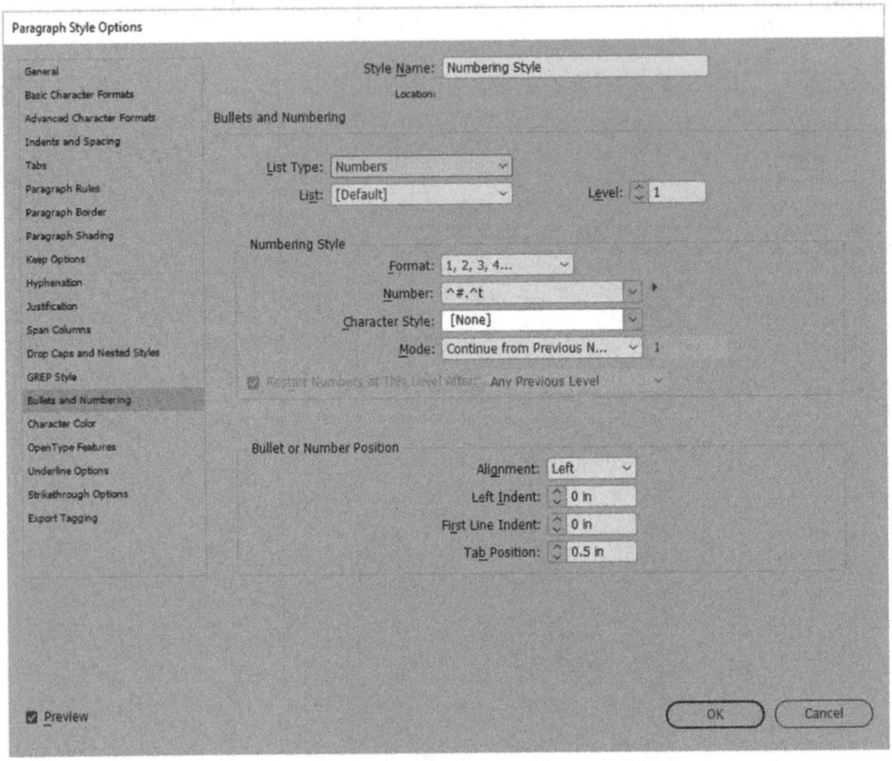

Figure 2-17. *Using the default Numbering Style settings in the Bullets and Numbering tab of the Paragraph Style Options dialog box*

1. Change the List Type to Numbers

2. Change the Numbering Style Format to 001, 002, 003 or 0001, 0002, 0003, whichever you prefer.

3. Next you need to make a few more adjustments. Under Numbering Style, the Number setting will originally have the code ^#.^t. This makes the normal bullet apply the order of 001., 002., 003., and so on, along with text. You want only the numbers, so just remove .^t, leaving ^# as shown in Figure 2-18. You can find more of these symbols in the drop-down list to the right of the Number field to adjust space and level. You will see more examples of this code in Chapter 6.

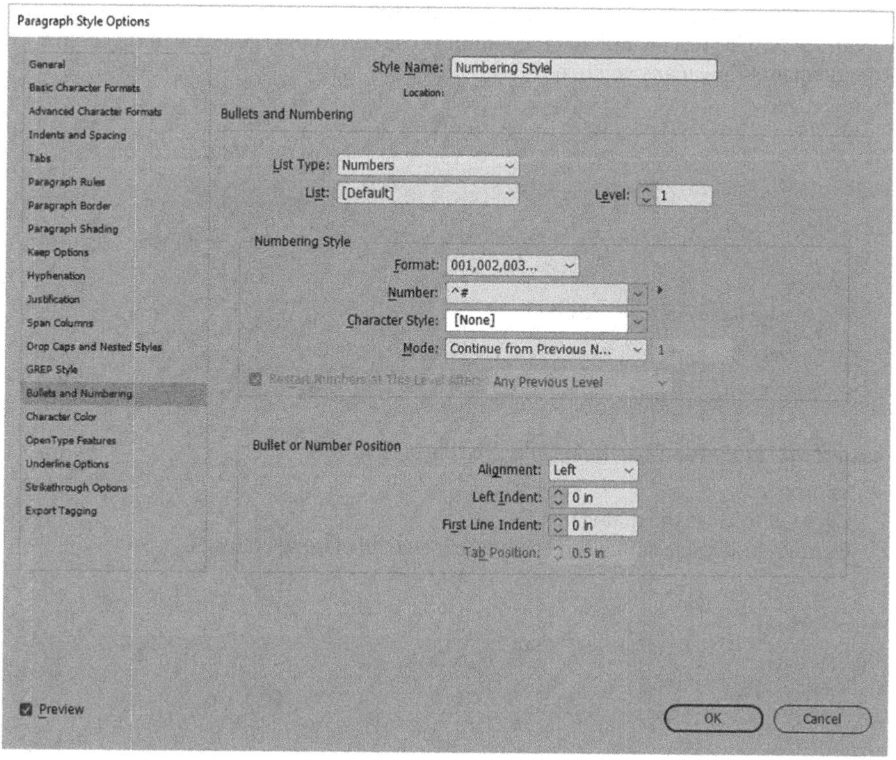

Figure 2-18. *Altering the Number settings and removing the decimal in the Bullets and Numbering tab of the Paragraph Style Options dialog box*

4. Leave the Mode setting at Continue from Previous Number, so that the number is unavailable.

■ **Note** If you need to start from 101, for example, change the number to start at 101. Switch the Mode setting back to Continue from Previous Number to make it unavailable. This refreshes the numbering so that the cycle will continue after 100. We'll look at that in detail later.

There is one last thing to change. Under the List Type drop-down, there is another drop-down called List. Choose New List, as shown in Figure 2-19.

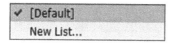

Figure 2-19. *The List drop-down menu on the Bullets and Numbering tab*

Name the new list Numbers. Make sure both available options are selected, as shown in Figure 2-20. This will ensure that the numbers will continue to generate in successive order no matter how many you need.

Figure 2-20. *In the New List dialog box, give the list a name*

Click OK to close the dialog box.
Figure 2-21 depicts a final screen shot reflected all of these changes.

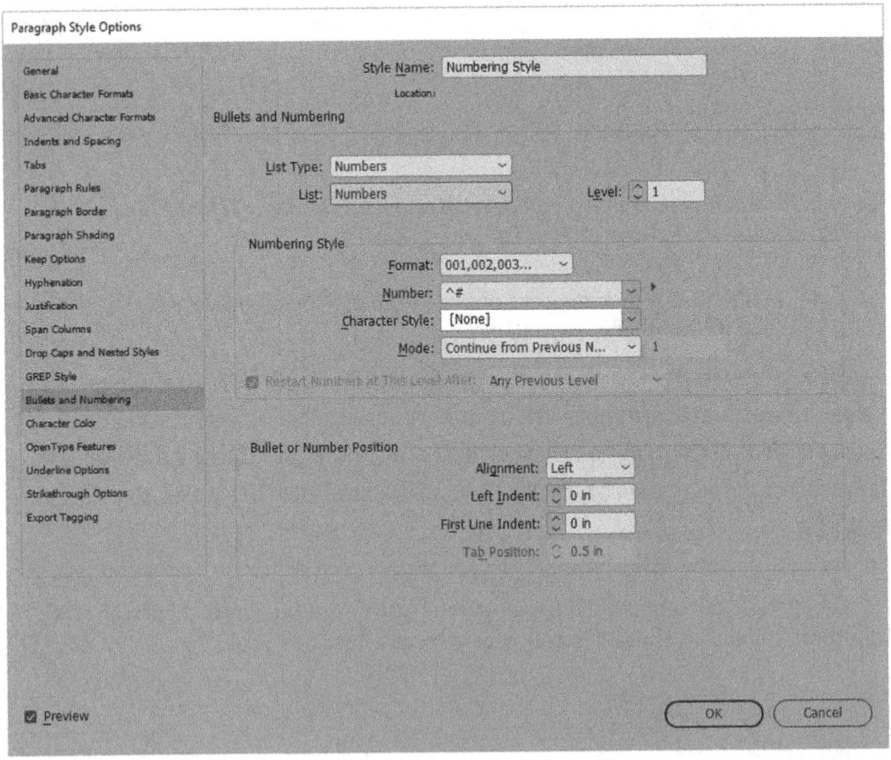

Figure 2-21. *The final revised settings on the Bullets and Numbering tab of the Paragraph Style Options dialog box.*

70

Click OK to confirm these changes and exit the Paragraph Styles dialog box.

Starting the Sequential Numbering

Click inside your text area and select the new Numbering Style to apply the changes, as shown in Figure 2-22.

Characte
Paragraph Styles
Numbering Style
[Basic Paragraph]
Numbering Style

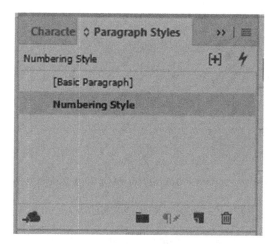

Figure 2-22. *The new Paragragh Style that is applied to the text box*

At first it will appear as if nothing has happened. Next, with the cursor in the text box, press the Enter key to make a paragraph return and the first number will appear, as shown in Figure 2-23.

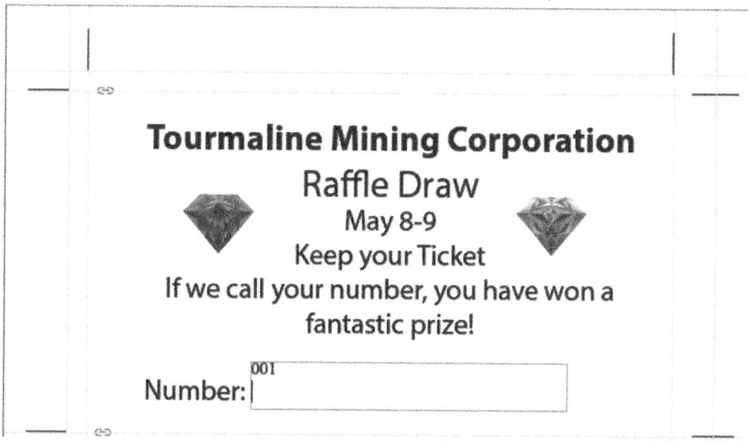

Tourmaline Mining Corporation
Raffle Draw
May 8-9
Keep your Ticket
If we call your number, you have won a
fantastic prize!
001
Number:

Figure 2-23. *The first number appears in the text box as 001*

If you find the number size too small, go back into your paragraph style by double-clicking it in the Paragraph Styles panel, shown in Figure 2-24.

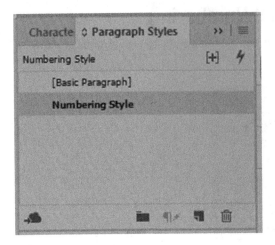

Figure 2-24. *Double-click Numbering Style to open the Paragraph Style Options dialog box*

Basic Character Formats Tab

You can use the Basic Character Formats tab to adjust the font style and size settings shown in Figure 2-25.

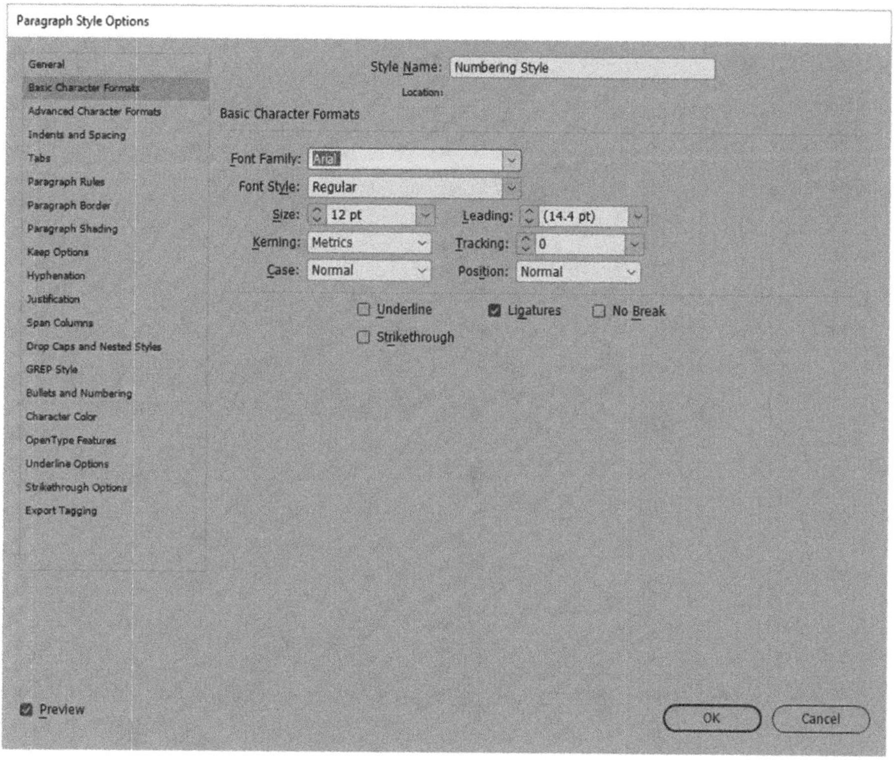

Figure 2-25. *The Basic Character Formats tab of the Paragraph Style Options dialog box*

The Basic Character Formats tab allows you to change settings like Font Family, Font Style, and Size, as well as other spacing adjustments like Leading, Kerning, and Tracking. You can set Case and Position, and add an underline, ligatures, a break, or strikethrough. For this exercise, make the following changes.

1. Set the Font Family to Arial or Helvetica.

2. Set the size to 12 pt and.

3. Set the leading to 14.4 pt.

Character Color Tab

The Character Color tab, shown in Figure 2-26, allows you to change a paragraph's color fill and stroke, tint, and weight, the miter limit for strokes, and its stroke alignment.

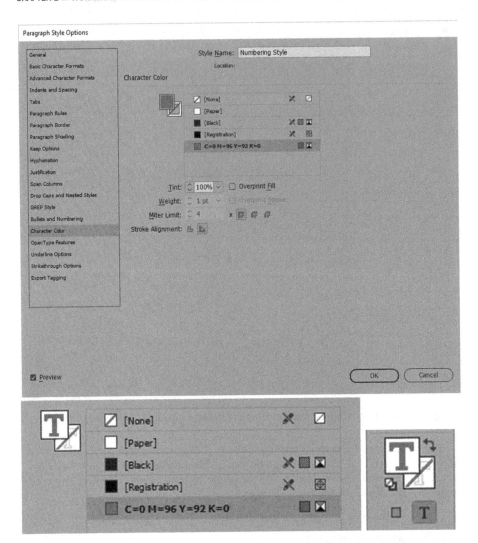

Figure 2-26. *The Character Color tab of the Paragraph Style Options dialog box. Note that if you have Formatting affect text tool (J) selected in the Tools panel, the icon will show up as a T. it will show up as a solid square if the formatted effect container is selected. Either way works while inside the dialog box.*

Change the Character Color to red. Click OK when done and exit the Paragraph Style options.

Other Optional Settings

Other tab options within the Paragraph Style Options dialog box that you could also adjust for your tickets include the following:

Advanced Character Formats Tab

On the Advanced Character Formats tab, shown in Figure 2-27, you can adjust the Horizontal Scale and Vertical Scale of the font. If you need it to be shaped a certain way, you could also adjust the skew if you wanted the number to look faux italic, for example.

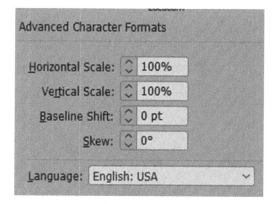

Figure 2-27. The Advanced Character Formats tab of the Paragraph Style Options dialog box

Indents and Spacing Tab

If you prefer the numbers to be aligned right or centered rather than the default of left, you can adjust that on the Indents and Spacing tab. You can also create a custom indent, as shown in Figure 2-28.

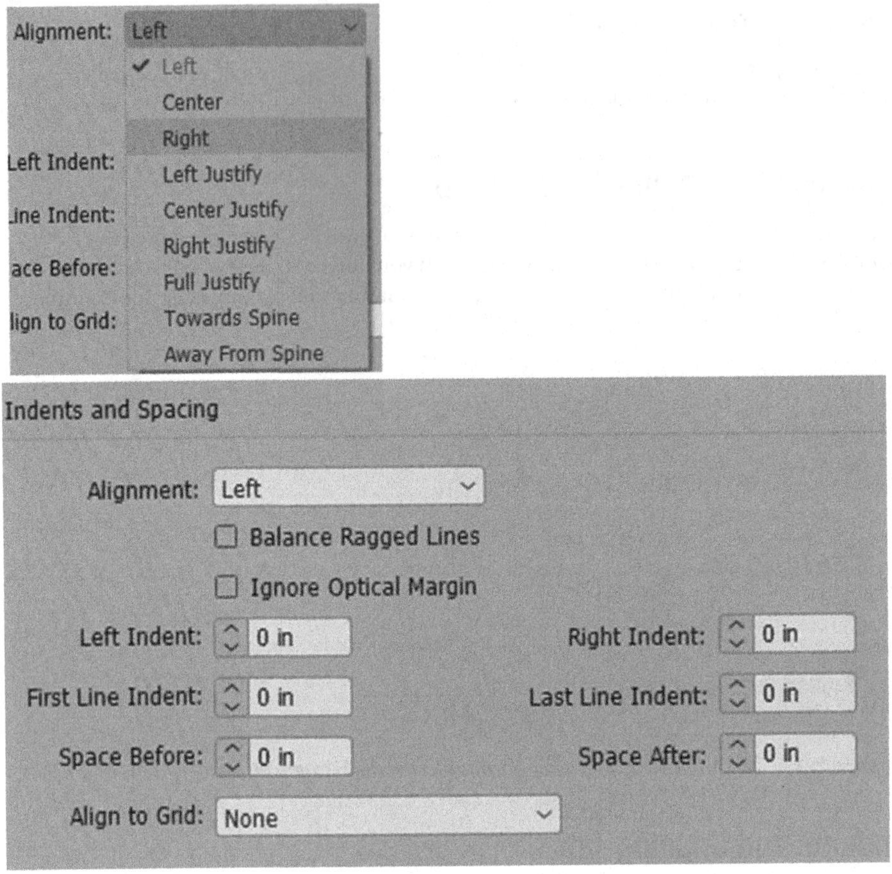

Figure 2-28. *The Indents and Spacing tab of the Paragraph Style Options dialog box*

Click OK to close the Paragraph Style Options dialog box. You will look at some other Paragraph Style options in later chapters.

For a detailed list of other Paragraph Style options, check out https://helpx.adobe. com/indesign/using/paragraph-character-styles.html. You can also refer to *Adobe InDesign CC Classroom in a Book.*

Adding Your Sequential Numbers to the Layout

With your black arrow Selection Tool (V) and arrow keys on your keyboard, move the text box around if you don't like the placement. You have now numbered the first ticket, as shown in Figure 2-29. However, there are still nine more on the sheet.

Figure 2-29. *The first number has been styled for the page*

With the Selection Tool (V), select the text box and hold down the Alt/Option Key to drag with your mouse a new copy of the text box for the ticket on the upper right side. When you drop it in the correct location, you will see that the number in the new duplicated box has changed to 002, as displayed in Figure 2-30. You might need to use the Align tools to make sure the numbers are balanced.

Figure 2-30. *After Alt + Mouse drag with the Selection Tool, you now have 2 linked numbers in the sequence*

The Align Panel

Go to Window ➤ Object & Layout ➤ Align (Shift + F7). This panel allows you to align selected text boxes or objects in set rows or columns. When you shift two or more selected boxes with your Selection Tool (V), while they are still selected, you can click the Align Top Edges icon, shown in Figure 2-31, and those items will be aligned by the top of their rectangular frame.

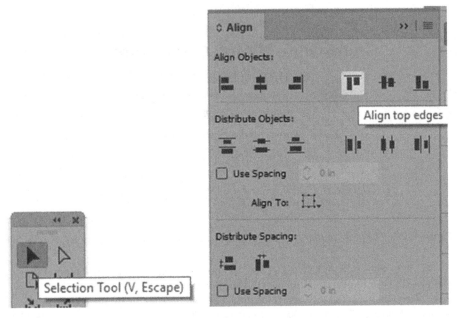

Figure 2-31. *Use the Align Panel to align the text boxes if they are not level with each other*

Continue to Alt/Option Drag with the Selection Tool until all the tickets on the page are numbered 001 to 010. You have now completed one page of tickets. Make sure to use the Align panel to make sure the boxes are aligned and appear as shown in Figure 2-32.

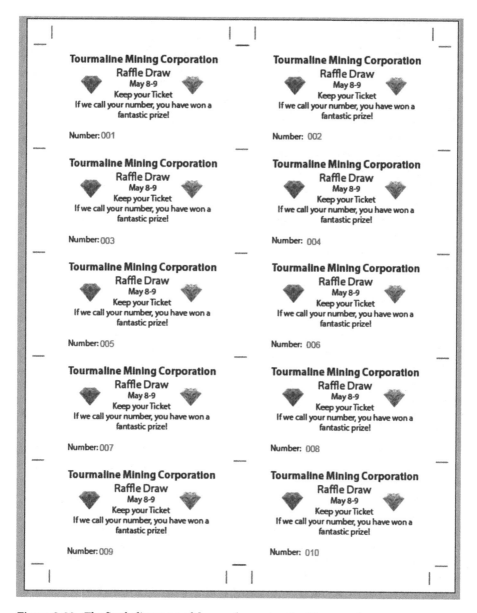

Figure 2-32. *The final alignment of the numbers using the Align panel*

The Pages Panel

In this example, you want 100 tickets. That means you need ten sheets or spreads because ten sheets of ten-up tickets results in 100 tickets.

You can continue the count by selecting the page or spread. Click Window ➤ Pages to open the Pages panel. This panel, shown in Figure 2-33, shows a thumbnail of all the pages in the document. Currently there is only one.

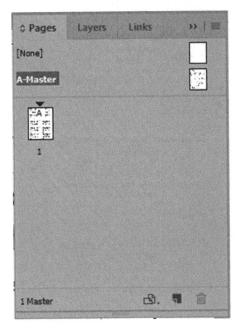

Figure 2-33. *The Pages panel displays the one page and the crop marks and graphics that are on the master page (A-Master)*

In this case, my graphics and crop marks are in A-Master. I did this so that if I needed to change my backgrounds I could easily do so in one area rather than making the change to each page. If you need to enter the A-Master, double-click the A-Master Icon in the Pages panel. To exit, click Page 1 in the Pages panel. Your Numbering Layer items should not be in the A-Master, but only on Page 1 for now.

Make sure you are on Page 1 and not in the A-Master by double-clicking on Page 1 Icon.

Right-click the page thumbnail and choose Duplicate Spread, as shown in Figure 2-34.

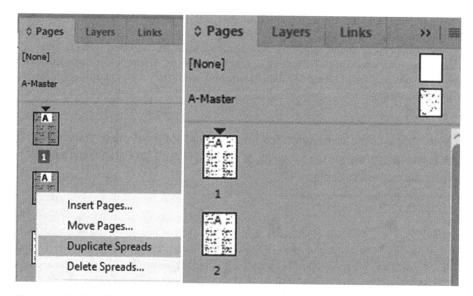

Figure 2-34. *Duplicating a spread in the Pages panel duplicates a page in the document*

Now you have 2 pages. Page 2 starts at number 011 and ends at 020.

Rather than just selecting one spread at a time and choosing Duplicate Spreads, you can hold down Shift, click both spreads, and choose Duplicate Spreads, as displayed in Figure 2-35. This makes two more spreads, so you have a total of four, now up to number 040.

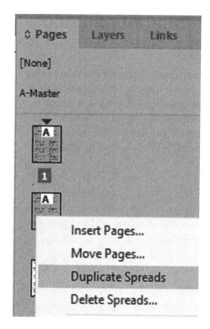

Figure 2-35. *Duplicating a spread by selecting more than one at a time speeds up the process*

Again, you can hold down Shift and click each one, repeating the same process and bringing you to a total of eight pages or 80 tickets.

You can press Shift and click the last two pages and select Duplicate Spreads. You should now have a total of 100 tickets or 10 sheets or spreads. At this point you could print the sheets out yourself or create a PDF of the file and send it to your local printer for them to print for you.

■ **Note** If you create too many spreads, select the ones at the end you don't want and click Delete Spread. You will see a warning, as shown in Figure 2-36. Click OK and the unwanted spread will be deleted.

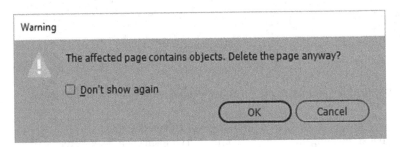

Figure 2-36. A warning that appears when you delete a page that contains content

Using Paragraph Styles to Continue Numbering from a New Number (Optional)

You can continue to use Paragraph Styles when you need more tickets for the same event.

Right before the event you might find out that you need to print 100 more tickets, bringing the count to 200. Do you have to create duplicates of more spreads or pages? No, all you need to do is start at the next numbering sequence. Without any text boxes selected, in the Paragraph Styles panel,select Numbering Style. Refer to Figure 2-24.

Go again to the Bullets and Numbering tab. Change the Mode setting to Start At and type 101 into the text box on the right (see Figure 2-37).

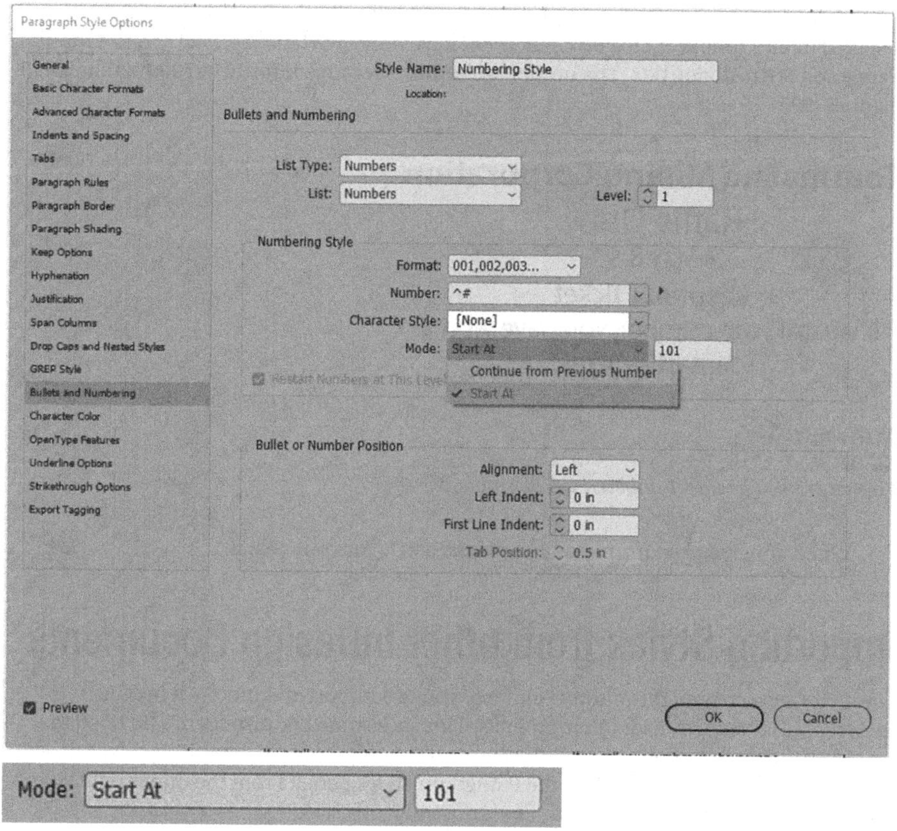

Figure 2-37. *On the Bullets and Numbering tab of the Paragraph Style Options dialog box, alter the number in the Mode setting to Start at and add a new number*

Next, change the Mode setting back to Continue from Previous Number to make the number unavailable, as seen in Figure 2-38.

Figure 2-38. *On the Bullets and Numbering tab of the Paragraph Style Options dialog box, alter the Mode setting to Continue from Previous Number to lock the new number in place. Stay in the dialog box and preview it until complete.*

Wait a few seconds for the numbers to recalculate with the Preview check box selected in the Options dialog box. Once you have previewed the file, click OK to exit the Paragraph Styles dialog box. The numbers should now range from 101 to 200, as shown in Figure 2-39.

Tourmaline Mining Corporation
Raffle Draw
May 8-9
Keep your Ticket
If we call your number, you have won a
fantastic prize!

Number: 200

Figure 2-39. *The last numbered ticket in the sequence*

When done you can print the file or make a PDF for your printer.

Importing Styles from other InDesign Documents

Once you have created this numbering style you can import and modify it in other InDesign CC documents for other projects. This saves time because there's no need to repeat all the steps again.

In your new document, open the Paragraph Styles panel. From the upper right side menu, select Load Paragraph Styles, as shown in Figure 2-40.

Load Paragraph Styles...
Load All Text Styles...

Figure 2-40. *From the menu in the Paragraph Styles panel, select Load Paragraph Styles*

Locate the file that contains your Numbering Style and click Open in the Open a File dialog box. You will then see the Load Styles dialog box. Select only the Numbering Style from the list and click OK, as shown in Figure 2-41.

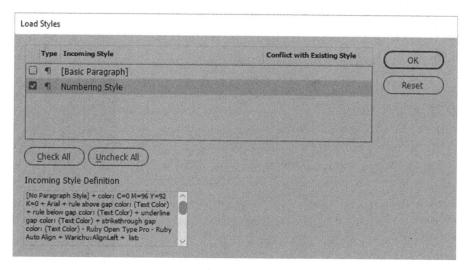

Figure 2-41. *The Load Styles dialog box*

This will load the Numbering Style into your new document (see Figure 2-42) and you can now use it in your own project when you apply it to your text box and press Enter to start the numbering sequence.

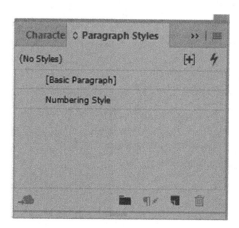

Figure 2-42. *The style is loaded into the new document*

Creating the Final PDF for Print

After you have saved your file, you might want to print it out directly from InDesign or create a PDF that you will e-mail to your print house.

To create a PDF, go to File ➤ Print and choose the following settings. On the General tab of the Print dialog box, set the settings shown in Figure 2-43.

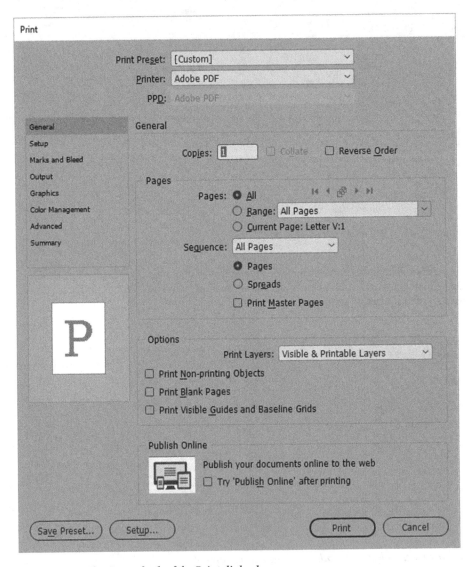

Figure 2-43. *The General tab of the Print dialog box*

On the Setup tab, make sure the Paper Size is set to Letter, or whatever layout size you are using. The Page Position should be set to Centered, as shown in Figure 2-44, to ensure that no parts of the image are cut off when the PDF is created.

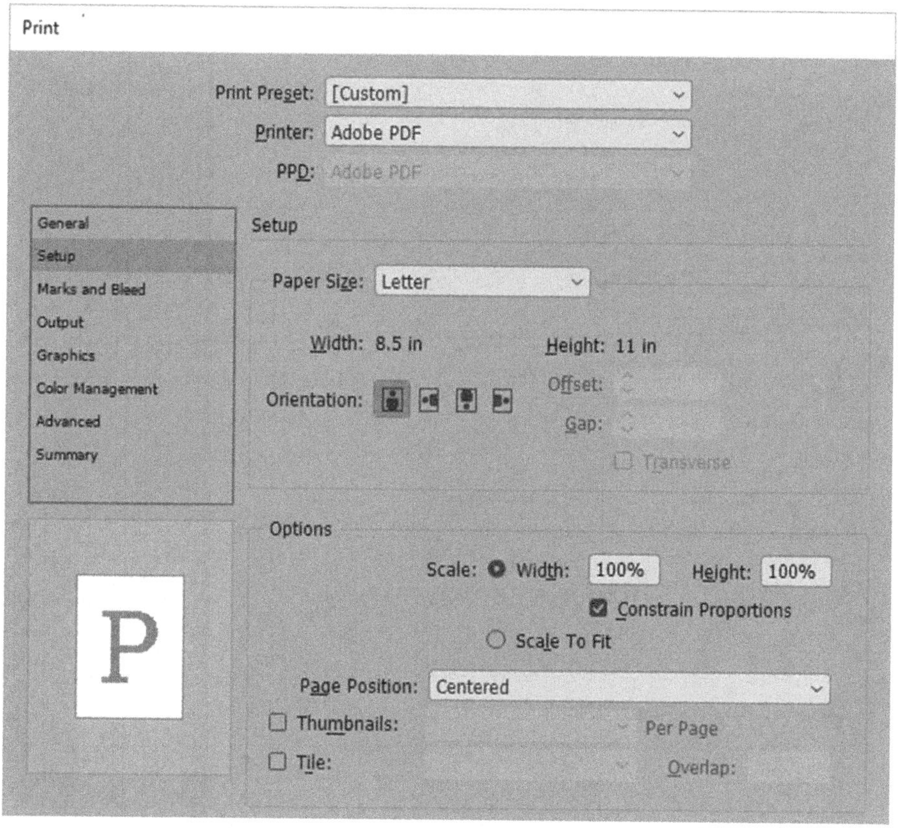

Figure 2-44. *The Setup tab of the Print dialog box*

On the Marks and Bleed tab, because I created my own custom layout, I will leave this set to the defaults with the All Printer's Mark check box cleared, as shown in Figure 2-45. Please check with your print house to see if they recommend any alternate adjustments here.

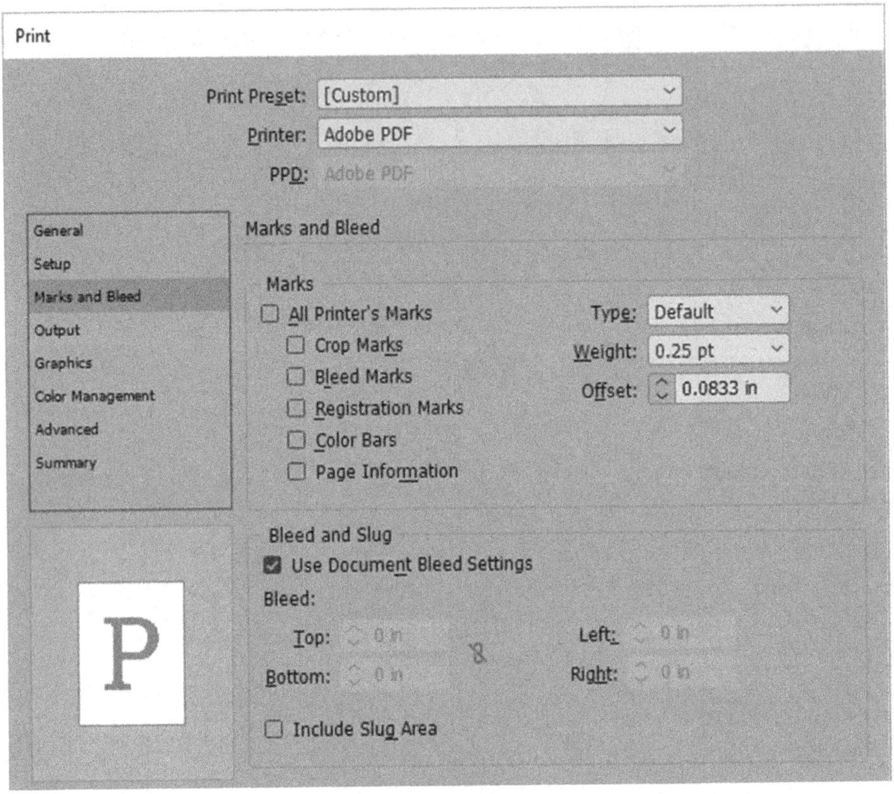

Figure 2-45. *The Marks and Bleed tab of the Print dialog box*

On the Output tab make sure that Color is set to Composite CMYK and that the Text as Black check box is cleared, as shown in Figure 2-46. Otherwise, leave everything at the defaults.

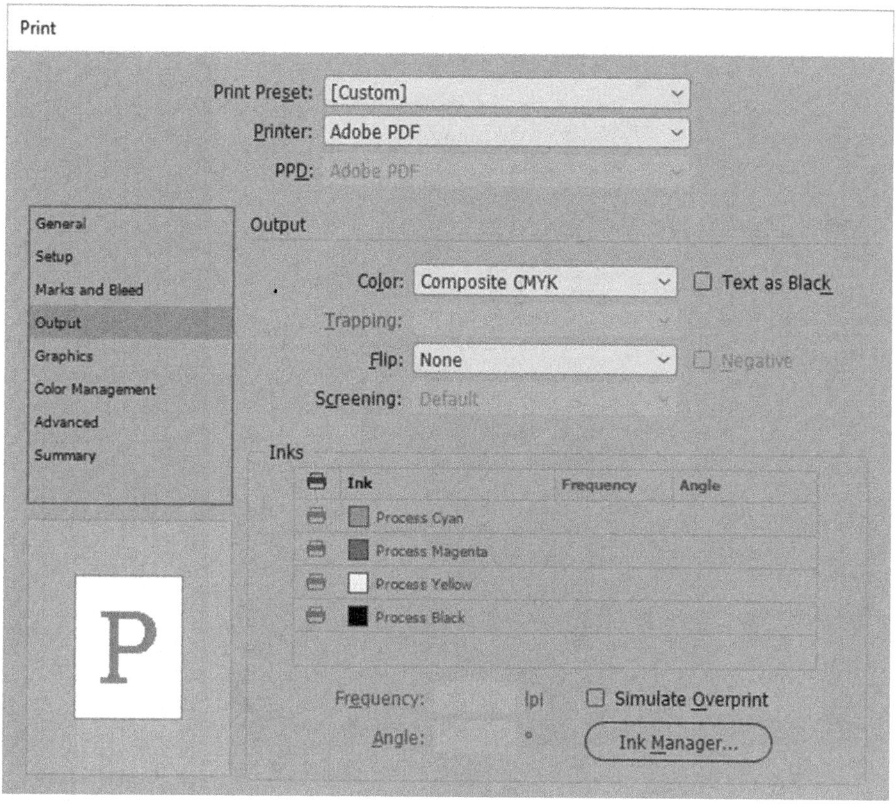

Figure 2-46. The Output tab of the Print dialog box

On the Graphics tab, set Send Data to All, because you want the images to be of decent quality. Under Font, set Download to Complete and PostScript should be set to Level 3, as depicted in Figure 2-47.

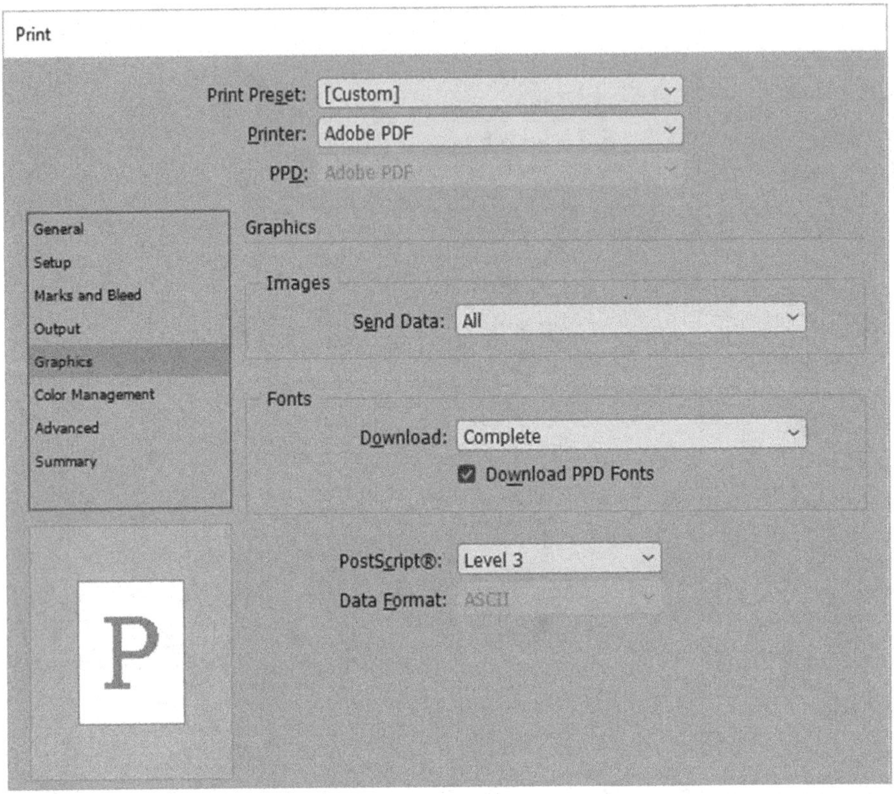

Figure 2-47. *The Graphics tab of the Print dialog box*

I generally leave the Color Management tab (see Figure 2-48) at the default settings and let InDesign determine the colors. However, your print house might have different settings they want you to use, so check with them.

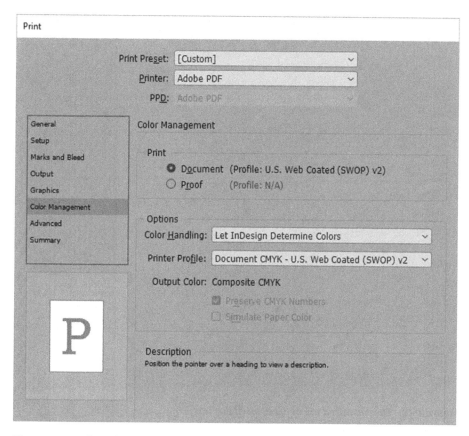

Figure 2-48. *The Color Managment tab of the Print dialog box*

Because you are not using any high-resolution graphics that need to replace low-resolution images, leave the Advanced tab, shown in Figure 2-49, at the default settings.

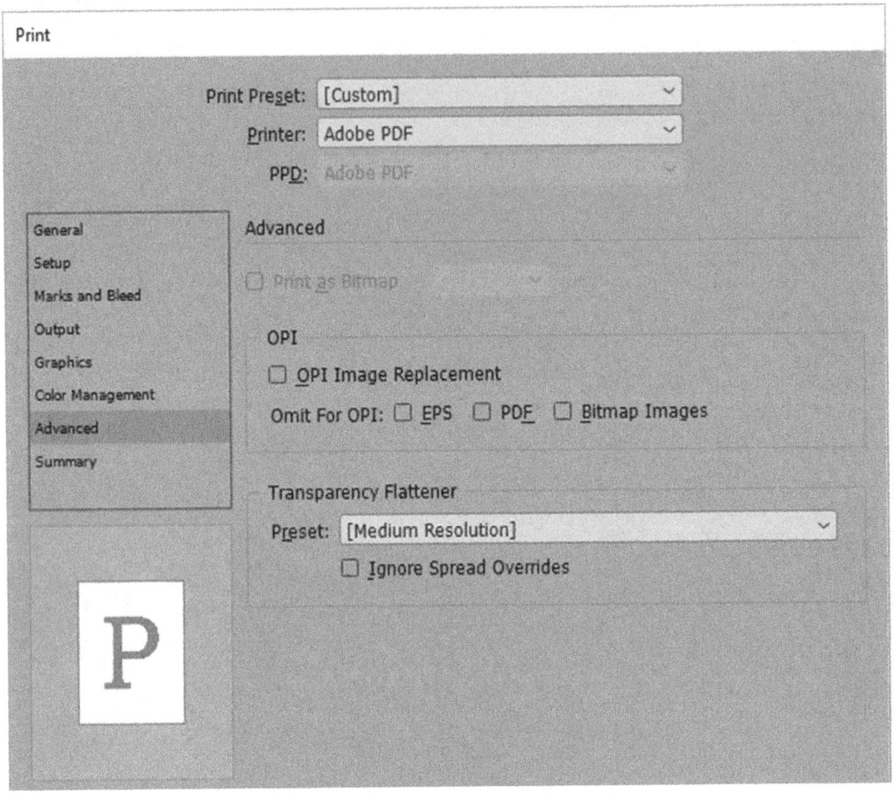

Figure 2-49. The Advanced tab of the Print dialog box

The Summary tab, depicted in Figure 2-50, also requires no changes.

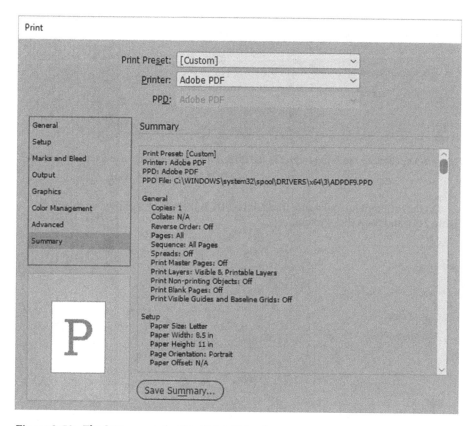

Figure 2-50. *The Summary tab of the Print dialog box*

Click Setup at the bottom of the Print dialog box, as shown in Figure 2-51.

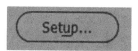

Figure 2-51. *The Setup Button in the Print dialog box*

The warning shown in Figure 2-52 will appear. Click OK.

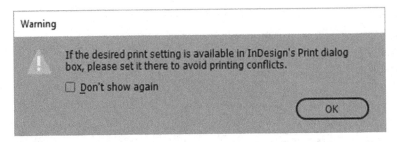

Figure 2-52. *Clicking the Setup button in the Print dialog box results in this warning message*

On the Print, menu make sure that Adobe PDF is the selected printer, as shown in Figure 2-53, and then click Preferences.

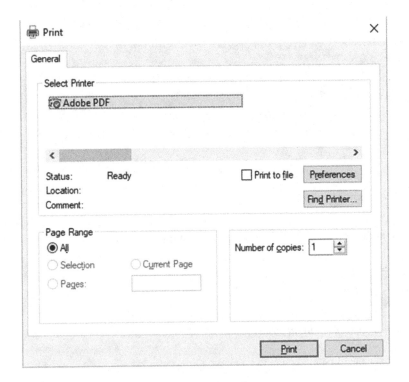

Figure 2-53. *Select Adobe PDF and click Preferences*

In the Printing Preferences dialog box, select High Quality Print or Standard from the Default Settings drop-down list shown in Figure 2-54. High quality will give you a larger file, but the graphics will look clearer. Standard will give you a smaller file size, but the graphics might appear fuzzy. Test to see which option works best for your layout.

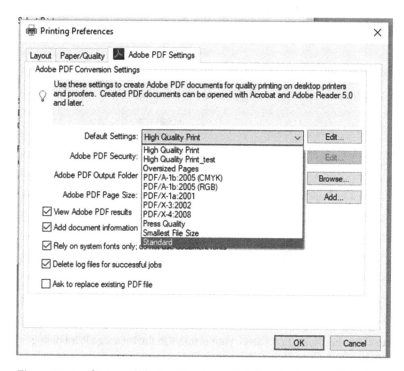

Figure 2-54. *Choose a default setting in the Printing Preferences dialog box*

Leave the other settings as is and click OK to close this dialog box. You will be returned to the Print dialog box shown in Figure 2-55.

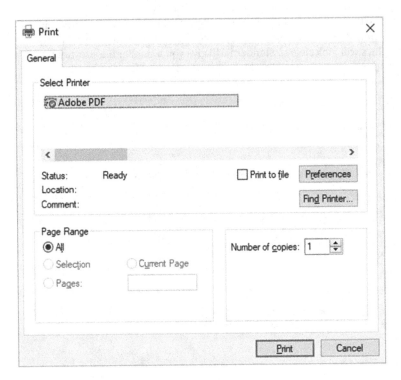

Figure 2-55. *In the Print dialog box, click Print*

Click Print to close this dialog box. Check your settings in the InDesign Print dialog box and click Print here as well, as shown in Figure 2-56.

Figure 2-56. *Click Print in the Print dialog box in Adobe InDesign CC*

Adobe Acrobat DC Distiller will now start creating the PDF.

Saving the PDF

Save the file in the desired location in your folder with a name reflecting the range of ticket numbers; for example, Raffle_10up_End_1_100 in Figure 2-57. This signifies tickets 1 to 100. You might have a different range. If you created another range later, giving the PDF a numbering like 101_200 will help you keep the various sets organized in case you need to send this new file to your printer at the last minute and they need to know what range this is.

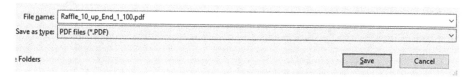

Figure 2-57. *Naming the file in the Print dialog box in Adobe InDesign CC*

Click Save. The PDF will be created and you can open it in Adobe Acrobat DC Pro to review and e-mail later.

Summary

In this chapter, you looked at how you can use Paragraph styles to enhance the layout of your ticket numbering. Although each of the numbers was different, each one still had a consistent look and coloring that coordinated with the layout. You also did not have to type out each number manually, which saved you time. In Chapter 5 you will revisit the raffle ticket again and see how you can add two sets of custom numbers and names using the Data Merge and you will look at another way in InDesign to se tup and create a PDF.

Before you can do this, though, you need to understand how to use the Data Merge panel. In the next chapter, you will first look at how to create a single merge record for a presentation letter for a mailing or conference.

■ ■ ■

Creating a Single Merge Record Using the Data Merge Panel

Project: Creating the Presentation Letter for Your Mailing

■ **Note**   If you want to work along in this lesson or review the result, download your Chapter 3 files from http://www.apress.com/9781484231586. Work with the file with the label "Start." The file with the label "End" and the PDFs are the final result.

The ability to number tickets is useful, but another handy tool is the Data Merge panel. As mentioned earlier, it is like the Mail Merge section of Microsoft Word. In InDesign, you might have created the layout for a one-page presentation letter for a folder. Within the layout of text, you will have set areas that will change like the name of the person or their address. In this chapter, I will show you how to achieve this using the Data Merge panel.

Working with the Data Merge Panel

To access the Data Merge panel, go to Window ➤ Utilities ➤ Data Merge. Like other panels, it has a shortcut menu on the right side. As you go through this lesson and the next chapters, you will look at each of the parts in this panel, which is shown in Figure 3-1.

© Jennifer Harder 2017
J. Harder, *Data Merge and Styles for Adobe InDesign CC 2018*,
https://doi.org/10.1007/978-1-4842-3159-3_3

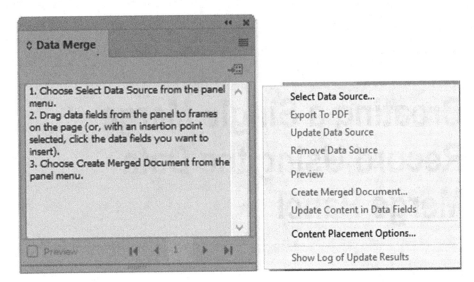

Figure 3-1. *The Data Merge panel and its menu options*

Open Adobe InDesign CC

To begin, open InDesign CC 2018. If you have not already set up your workspace, make sure to go back to Chapter 1 and review the information on creating a workspace for the Data Merge. Otherwise, select the Data Merge Workspace or Reset Data Merge Workspace from the InDesign drop-down menu now, as shown in Figure 3-2.

Figure 3-2. *The Data Merge Workspace shown on the workspace's drop-down menu*

If you were beginning the files from scratch, you would choose File ➤ New Document and begin laying out the text and graphics that you might have created in Photoshop or Illustrator. However, for this chapter, choose File ➤ Open to open the document (Presentation_Start_1.indd) in the Chapter 3 folder, which is the file that contains the layout I have already created.

Creating a Spreadsheet in Excel and Saving It as a CSV File for InDesign

To create custom text for a cover letter, you need a document that you created in InDesign and a .csv file that was created in Microsoft Excel. InDesign cannot use .xlsx or Excel extensions, so files must be only comma-delimited (.csv) or tab-delimited (.txt) files. If you have an Excel file already created, you need to convert it to a .csv file.

A comma-delimited file is separated by commas when viewed in text form in a program like Notepad++. For example:

> FirstName,LastName,Age

> Jackie,Smith,40

> Mary,Jones,45

Let's explore how to do that. Open your Excel spreadsheet, Employee_List.xlsx. In your case, it might have been created from a database or you migh have typed it yourself. Make sure on you have clear headings for each column on the first line, as shown in Figure 3-3.

	A	B	C	D	E	F	G	H	I	J
1	FirstName	LastName	Title	Address	City	Province	PostalCode	Employee Number	Phone Number	Email
2	John	Smith	CEO	444 West Elm Street	Vancouver	BC	V9K 4B7	2121	604-999-5542	jsmith@tmc.com
3	Mary	Lewis	HR Manager	343 East Garnet Ave	Burnaby	BC	V3T 4R9	1311	604-333-4567	mlewis@tmc.com
4	Cody	Thompson	Chief Engineer	564 Begbie Way	Revelstoke	BC	V8T 4J5	2122	878-673-5532	cthompson@tmc.com
5	Alex	Jackson	Chief Surveyor	563 Begbie Way	Revelstoke	BC	V8T 4J8	2123	878-673-5532	ajackson@tmc.com
6	Jana	Martins	Administration	676 Northroad Drive	Calgary	AB	V5T 4Q8	2125	605-676-4564	jmartins@tmc.com
7	Nancy	Coleman	Accountant	453 Cooper Lane	Surrey	BC	V6R 2T1	2454	604-676-3433	ncoleman@tmc.com
8	Jackie	Vadder	Graphic Designer	444 West Elm Street	Vancouver	BC	V5K 4B7	2456	604-999-5543	jvadder@tmc.com
9	Carol	Harper	Geologist	676 Blackrock Ave	Vancouver	BC	V5Q 8T4	2563	604-556-9786	charper@tmc.com
10	George	Walters	Geologist	454 Jade Ave	Revelstoke	BC	V6T 5T8	2453	604-567-3433	gwalters@tmc.com
11	Jason	Cruz	Mine Manager	454 Jade Ave	Revelstoke	BC	V6T 5T8	5655	676-909-7878	jcruz@tmc.com
12	Gordy	Barker	Safety Officer	454 Jade Ave	Revelstoke	BC	V6T 5T8	1124	778-668-5653	gbarker@tmc.com
13	Philippe	Pétain	Prospector	343 Bluemud Drive	Revelstoke	BC	V5Q 9T4	4456	778-999-5651	ppetain@tmc.com

Figure 3-3. *The Excel spreadsheet with all of the fields filled in*

Click File ➤ Save As, and select CSV (comma delimited), as shown in Figure 3-4. Do not save it as a CSV UTF-8 file, as this format will not work.

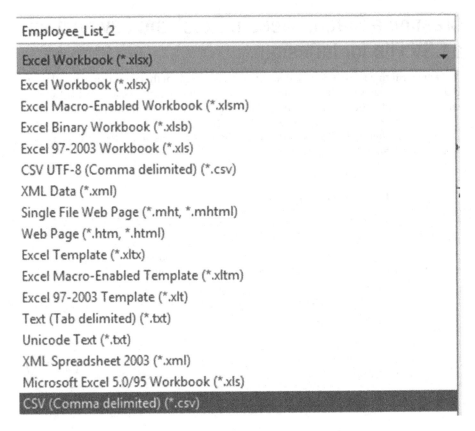

Figure 3-4. *Choose CSV (Comma delimited)(*.csv)from the list of choices*

Click Save. You might get a warning from Excel, like the one shown in Figure 3-5. Click OK.

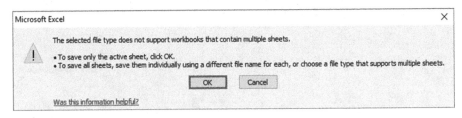

Figure 3-5. *Warning that this file does not support certain features anymore*

The file should now be saved as a .csv file. Close the CSV file in Excel.

■ **Note** Be sure that if your names have special character accents that they do not get removed; for example, French names like Philippe Pétain.

If this happens, when you go to Save as, click the More Options link (refer to Figure 3-6).

Figure 3-6. *When you save the file, click the More Options link*

Enter the name you want to give the file and choose CSV (Comma delimited) as the file type.

In the Tools drop-down menu, select Web Options, as shown in Figure 3-7.

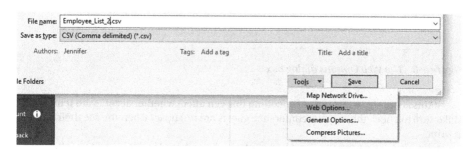

Figure 3-7. *Choose Tools* ➤ *Web Options before saving the file*

Click the Encoding tab and make sure the Save This Document drop-down list is set to Unicode (UTF-8), as shown in Figure 3-8.

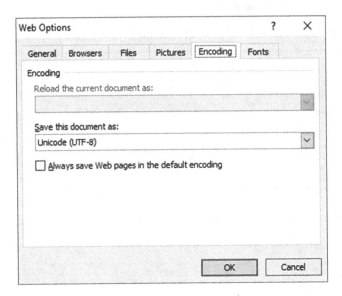

Figure 3-8. *The Web Options dialog box*

If this is not set to this type of encoding this can affect whether accents are removed. Make sure to check this so your conference guests are not upset when the see their names in print.

Next, click OK to exit the Excel Web Options dialog box. The file should now be named EmployeeList_2.csv. Click Save. The accent on the name should now be retained in the CSV file. Close Excel and any of its open files.

Laying Out the InDesign File Cover Letter

In InDesign CC, have the PresentationStart_1.indd file open to view. This cover letter is shown in Figure 3-9.

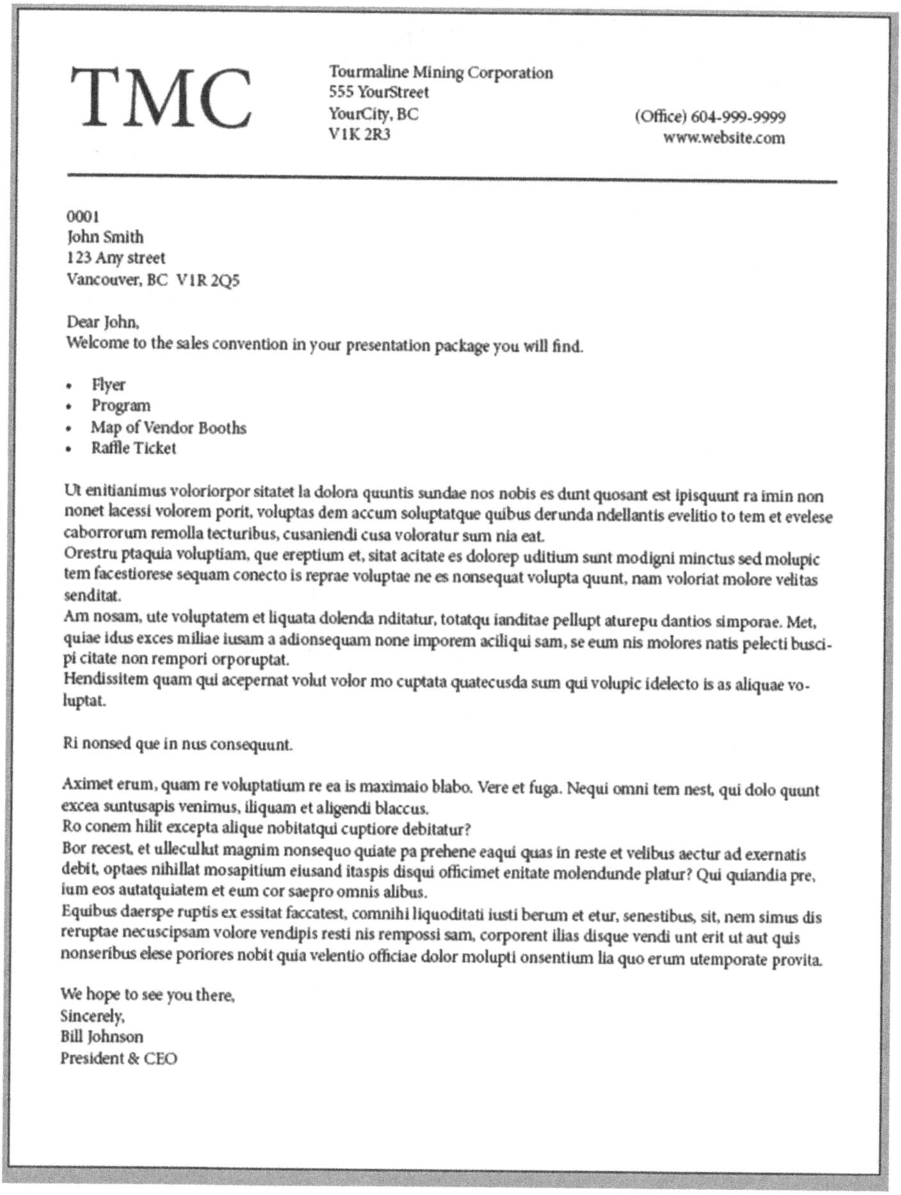

TMC

Tourmaline Mining Corporation
555 YourStreet
YourCity, BC   (Office) 604-999-9999
V1K 2R3   www.website.com

0001
John Smith
123 Any street
Vancouver, BC V1R 2Q5

Dear John,
Welcome to the sales convention in your presentation package you will find.

- Flyer
- Program
- Map of Vendor Booths
- Raffle Ticket

Ut enitianimus voloriorpor sitatet la dolora quuntis sundae nos nobis es dunt quosant est ipisquunt ra imin non nonet lacessi volorem porit, voluptas dem accum soluptatque quibus derunda ndellantis evelitio to tem et evelese caborrorum remolla tecturibus, cusaniendi cusa voloratur sum nia eat.
Orestru ptaquia voluptiam, que ereptium et, sitat acitate es dolorep uditium sunt modigni minctus sed molupic tem facestiorese sequam conecto is reprae voluptae ne es nonsequat volupta quunt, nam voloriat molore velitas senditat.
Am nosam, ute voluptatem et liquata dolenda nditatur, totatqu ianditae pellupt aturepu dantios simporae. Met, quiae idus exces miliae iusam a adionsequam none imporem aciliqui sam, se eum nis molores natis pelecti busci-pi citate non rempori orporuptat.
Hendissitem quam qui acepernat volut volor mo cuptata quatecusda sum qui volupic idelecto is as aliquae vo-luptat.

Ri nonsed que in nus consequunt.

Aximet erum, quam re voluptatium re ea is maximaio blabo. Vere et fuga. Nequi omni tem nest, qui dolo quunt excea suntusapis venimus, iliquam et aligendi blaccus.
Ro conem hilit excepta alique nobitatqui cuptiore debitatur?
Bor recest, et ulleculkut magnim nonsequo quiate pa prehene eaqui quas in reste et velibus aectur ad exernatis debit, optaes nihillat mosapitium eiusand itaspis disqui officimet enitate molendunde platur? Qui quiandia pre, ium eos autatquiatem et eum cor saepro omnis alibus.
Equibus daerspe ruptis ex essitat faccatest, comnihi liquoditati iusti berum et etur, senestibus, sit, nem simus dis reruptae necuscipsam volore vendipis resti nis rempossi sam, corporent ilias disque vendi unt erit ut aut quis nonseribus elese poriores nobit quia velentio officiae dolor molupti onsentium lia quo erum utemporate provita.

We hope to see you there,
Sincerely,
Bill Johnson
President & CEO

Figure 3-9. *The presentation letter*

You should save a copy of this file before you begin the Data Merge in case you need to go back and practice again. Click File ➤ Save As PresentationMerge_1.indd, and save the file in your Chapter 3 folder.

Working with the Data Merge Panel and Dialog Box

Go to Window ➤ Utilities Data ➤ Merge. With the Data Merge panel open, select Select Data Source from the shortcut menu on the right side, as shown in Figure 3-10.

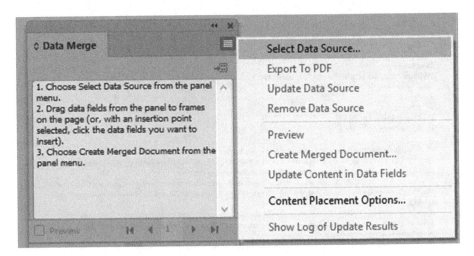

Figure 3-10. In the Data Merge panel, select Select Data Source

Locate the Employee_List_2.csv file in your folder and click Open. All the headings that were in the original Excel file will appear in the CSV file and be connected via the Data Merge panel, as displayed in Figure 3-11.

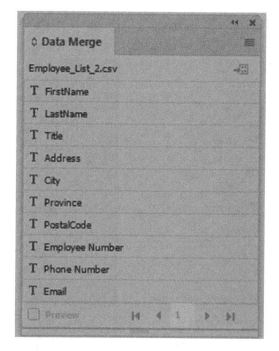

Figure 3-11. *The headings from the CSV file appear in the Data Merge panel*

The Data Merge panel now lists the cells you can use for your merge.

Inserting Data into the Presentation Letter by Working with the Data Source

In your InDesign layout with your Type tool, drag and highlight the Employee Number in the Address field, as shown in Figure 3-12.

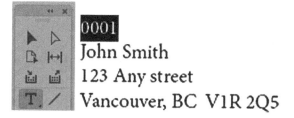

Figure 3-12. *Highlighting the employee number*

107

While it is highlighted, click Employee Number in the Data Merge panel, as shown in Figure 3-13.

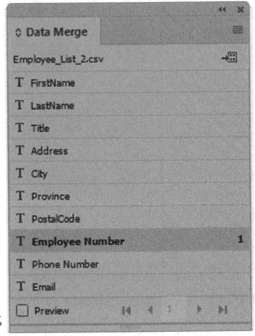

Figure 3-13. The Employee Number is now set and linked to the Data Merge panel

Next highlight the text John in the Address field. Click FirstName in the Data Merge panel, as shown in Figure 3-14.

<<Employee Number>>
John Smith
123 Any street
Vancouver, BC V1R 2Q5

<<Employee Number>>
<<FirstName>> Smith
123 Any street
Vancouver, BC V1R 2Q5

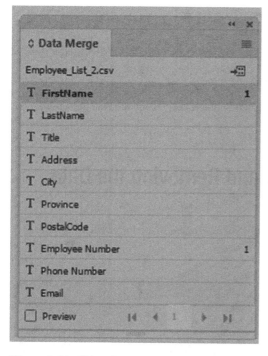

Figure 3-14. *Using the Data Merge panel to link the first name in the address*

Continue with LastName and so on, until it looks like this Figure 3-15.

<<Employee Number>>
<<FirstName>> <<LastName>>
<<Address>>
<<City>>, <<Province>> <<PostalCode>>

Dear <<FirstName>>,

Figure 3-15. *The completed data merge in the letter*

■ **Note** If you aren't sure if you have a space between the first and last names, you can use Type ➤ Show Hidden Characters (Ctrl+Alt+I) to see if there is a space, as displayed in Figure 3-16.

<<FirstName>>·<<LastName>>¶

Figure 3-16. The first and last name have a space between them indicated by a blue dot when shown in Hidden Character mode

After you are done, select Type ➤ Hide Hidden Characters and continue with the lesson.

Previewing, Updating, and Removing the Data Source

To see if the names are displaying correctly, check Preview in the lower left area of the Data Merge panel, as shown in Figure 3-17.

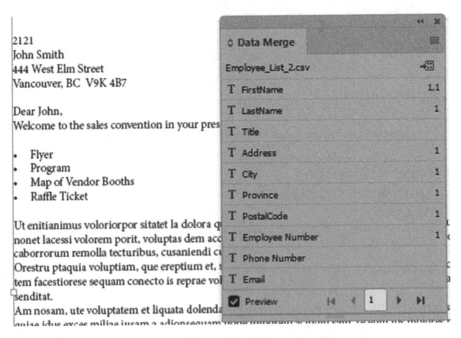

Figure 3-17. Using the Preview check box and arrows to review the names

You can then use the lower arrows in the panel to see the first name, previous name, next name, and last name. You can even type in the number of any record you choose. Use the Preview function to scroll through using the arrows to determine if all the names are appearing correctly.

At some point in your own project, you might notice a name or address is wrong. Go back to the original Excel file, open it in Excel, and correct the mistake. Resave the file as a new CSV file with the same name as mentioned in the earlier steps.

To refresh, you must now select Update the Data Source or you could remove it entirely (select Remove Data Source) and then Select Data Source again. In this case, select Update Data Source, as shown in Figure 3-18.

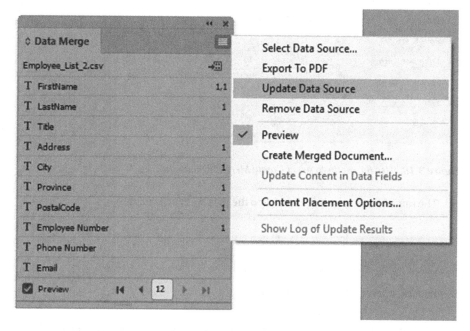

Figure 3-18. *In the Data Merge panel, select Update Data Source when information in the CSV changes so that the changes will be reflected in InDesign*

After you update the file, you can recheck the Preview again to make sure the update has taken effect when you review the record.

Creating a Single Merge Record Document for a One-Page File

Once you're happy with the results, it's time to make a merged document of multiple letters. To do so, choose Create Merged Document from the panel. Refer to Figures 3-19 and 3-20.

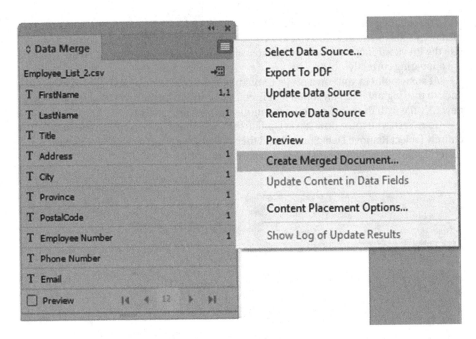

Figure 3-19. Use the menu to select Create Merged Document

The same button icon is found next to the data source file name.

Figure 3-20. Create Merged Document icon.

When you select Create Merged Document or click the Create Merged Document button, the Create Merged Document dialog box opens, as shown in Figure 3-21.

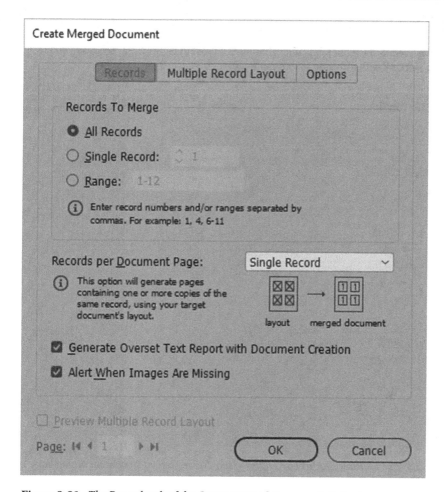

Figure 3-21. *The Records tab of the Create Merged Document dialog box*

The Records Tab

On the Records tab, in this case, you are going to select All Records. If you don't want to print everything, you could choose Single Record or Range to print a selected range of records.

Leave the Records per Document Page set to Single Record. Multiple records would be used when you have more than one record name on a page, as you'll see in Chapter 5.

Use the Generate Overset Text Report with Document Creation check box to specify that a Text Overset Report will generate if some text was more than the box could hold. If this is the case, you might need go back to the file to adjust the size of the box to hold the text or adjust the Paragraph or Character styles of the font, as you will see in a later chapter.

You can also add images through the Data Merge so you can be alerted if the images are missing. You will look at this area in more detail in Chapter 4.

Multiple Record Layout Tab

The Multiple Record Layout tab is unavailable, as shown in Figure 3-22, because you are currently working with only one record per page.

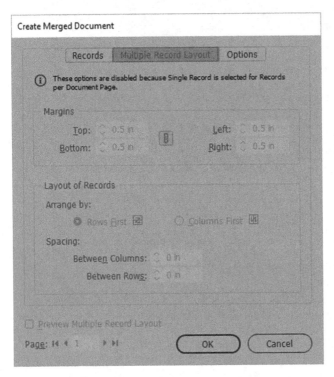

Figure 3-22. *The Multiple Record Layout tab of the Create Merged Document dialog box*

Options Tab

If there are images, you can control how they will appear on the Options tab, shown in Figure 3-23. For now, leave these settings at their defaults. You'll look at this area in Chapter 4.

Create Merged Document

| Records | Multiple Record Layout | Options |

Image Placement

Fitting: Fit Images Proportionally ⌄

☐ Center In Frame

☑ Link Images

☐ Remove Blank Lines for Empty Fields

☐ Record Limit per Document: 50

☐ Preview Multiple Record Layout

Page: |◄ ◄ 1 ► ►| (OK)   (Cancel)

Figure 3-23. *The Options tab of the Create Merged Document dialog box*

Once you're done, click OK to start the merge process. Give InDesign time to create the new merged document if you have a lot of records. If all is working, you should see the message shown in Figure 3-24 and a new document with the file name and a -1 on the end.

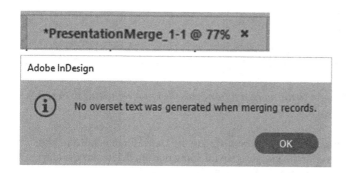

*PresentationMerge_1-1 @ 77% ✕

Adobe InDesign

ⓘ   No overset text was generated when merging records.

OK

Figure 3-24. *The Data Merge File is created and an alert is generated to let you know that no overset text was generated during the merge*

Click OK. You should now have one page for each record created, in this case 12 pages, as displayed in Figure 3-25.

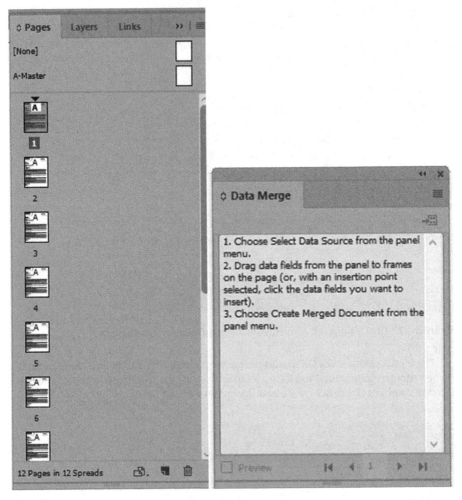

Figure 3-25. *There are 12 pages in the merged file and this file is not connected to the Data Merge panel*

Note that this newly created file is not connected to the Data Merge panel and is ready for print. If you need to run the merge again for some reason, delete this file and run the merge again from the original file, Presentation Merge_1.indd.

You can save this new file, even edit it, and print it or make a PDF to send to your print house.

Creating a Final PDF for Print or Export to PDF

If you are creating the file for your print house, I would recommend that you first create the InDesign file. If you find overset text, correct it and follow the steps that I outlined in Chapter 2 for setting up the Print dialog box for a PDF file. However, if you discover no overset text, you can reach a similar Print dialog box another way. Use the Data Merge panel and select Export to PDF, as shown in Figure 3-26.

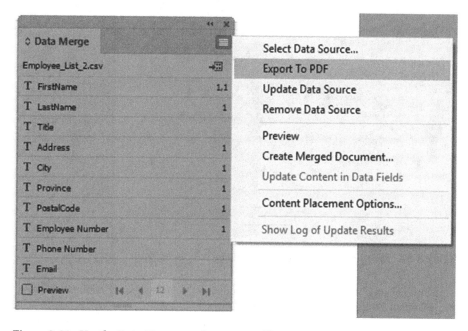

Figure 3-26. *Use the Data Merge panel to export a file to a PDF*

This will open the same Create Merged Document dialog box again, shown in Figure 3-27

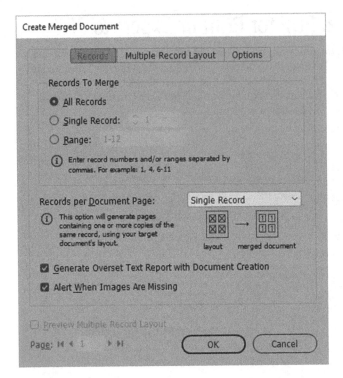

Figure 3-27. *The Create Merged Document dialog box opens again*

However, after you adjust your settings and click OK, a new Export Adobe PDF dialog box will open, as shown in Figure 3-28.

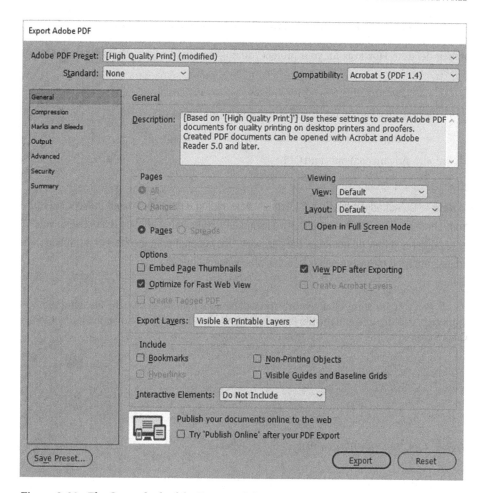

Figure 3-28. *The General tab of the Export Adobe PDF dialog box*

▪ **Note** If you choose to use this method of creating a PDF for your files in Chapter 2, you can access this same dialog box through File ➤ Export, and choose the file type PDF (Print). Find the location to which you want to save the file and then click OK. This will bring up the same dialog box shown in Figure 3-28. Although both methods work well, they do not contain the same tabs. For example, the Setup tab is found in Chapter 2. Choose the method that fits your workflow for PDF creations.

On the General tab, the only area you cleared was Bookmarks. Make sure that Adobe PDF Preset is set to [High Quality Print]. The settings on the other tabs should be left at their defaults. However, for your project you might want to adjust other tabs such as these:

- Compression: Setting for images.

- Marks and Bleeds: Crop marks and printer marks.

- Output: This controls color and the Ink Manager.

- Advanced: Fonts and OPI.

■ **Note**   Do not adjust the Security tab because adding a password might prevent the PDF from printing. Leave this area alone. If you send a PDF file with a printing restriction to your local printer and they do not know the password, they cannot print the file. For a printing project, applying password settings to this area wastes time.

When you are done, click Export. You will be asked where to save the file. Find the appropriate folder and call the file `PresentationMerge_1a.pdf`, as shown in Figure 3-29. Click Save.

Figure 3-29. Save the file as a PDF

InDesign will again alert you that no overset text was generated with the message shown in Figure 3-30.

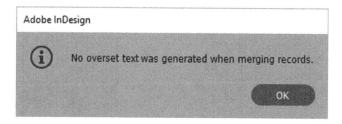

Figure 3-30. *If no overset text was generated you will see this message*

Click OK, and the PDF will appear in Adobe Acrobat DC for you to review all 12 records.

Single Merge Record Documents That Are More Than One Page

In some cases, a presentation letter might be on two or more pages, and you might want to separate these letters to send as an e-mail to each client later. Is there any way to do this?

Yes, there is. Open the file PresentationMerge_2.indd. In this case, the letter is two pages long and there is another Data Merge record of the first name somewhere on page 2, as indicated in Figure 3-31.

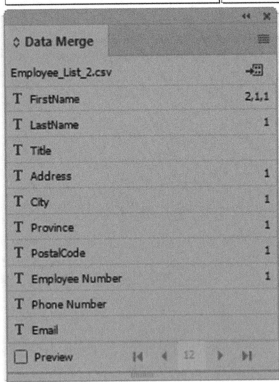

Figure 3-31. The Data Merge panel indicates that somewhere on page 2 there is another record

For this file you will again open the Create Merged Document dialog box as shown in Figure 3-32.

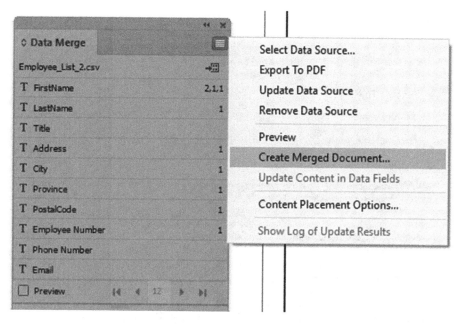

Figure 3-32. The Data Merge panel, selecting Create Merged Document

After you have adjusted your settings on the Records tab, click OK as shown in Figure 3-33.

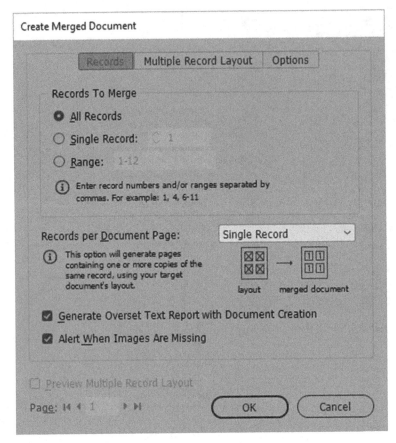

Figure 3-33. *The Records tab of the Create Merged Document dialog box*

This time the Data Merge has created a file that is 24 pages long for the 12 records. Page 1 of the document and page 2 of the document follow each other for each record set, as shown in Figure 3-34.

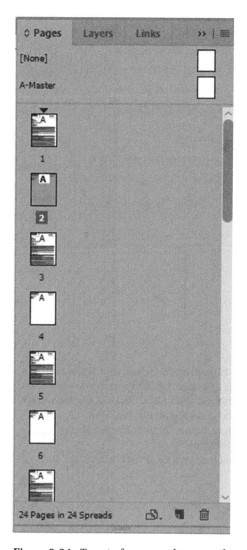

Figure 3-34. *Twenty-four pages have now been generated for the 12 records*

So how do you now make each file separate so that you can e-mail or mail them to the correct person? Close the file without saving it.

Go back to PresentationMerge_2.indd. In the Data Merge panel, again choose Export to PDF, as displayed in Figure 3-35.

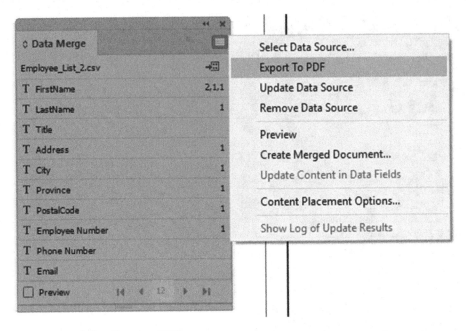

Figure 3-35. *Select Export to PDF*

The Create Merge Document dialog box will open again. Adjust your Record settings and click OK. The Export Adobe PDF dialog box will open. Click Export as you saw earlier.

Save your file as `PresentationMerge_2a.pdf` and click Save. Click OK for the overset text alert and a PDF with 24 pages will be created in Adobe Acrobat DC Pro.

Now you can print the PDF either as one long document in Adobe Acrobat using File ➤ Print, or you can extract the letters as individual files.

In Adobe Acrobat DC, while your PDF is open go to Tools ➤ Organize Pages Tool. Refer to Figure 3-36.

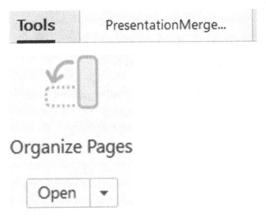

Figure 3-36. *In Adobe Acrobat you can use the Organize Pages tool to extract or split records*

When you click the Organize Pages tool, you will be presented with thumbnails of all the pages, as shown in Figure 3-37.

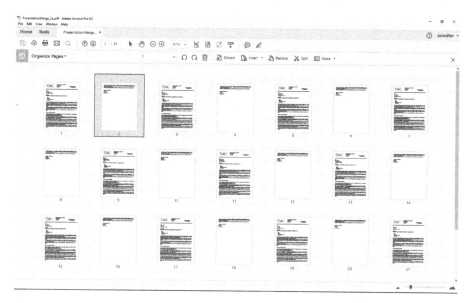

Figure 3-37. *The Organize Pages tool*

In the Organize Pages area, click the Split tool, shown in Figure 3-38.

Figure 3-38. *The Split tool*

Several options will appear, as depicted in Figure 3-39.

Figure 3-39. *Options for the Split tool*

Choose Split by: Number of pages: 2 pages and check the settings in the Output Options dialog box. I left mine at the default settings, but you might want to alter the labeling for your files, as shown in Figure 3-40.

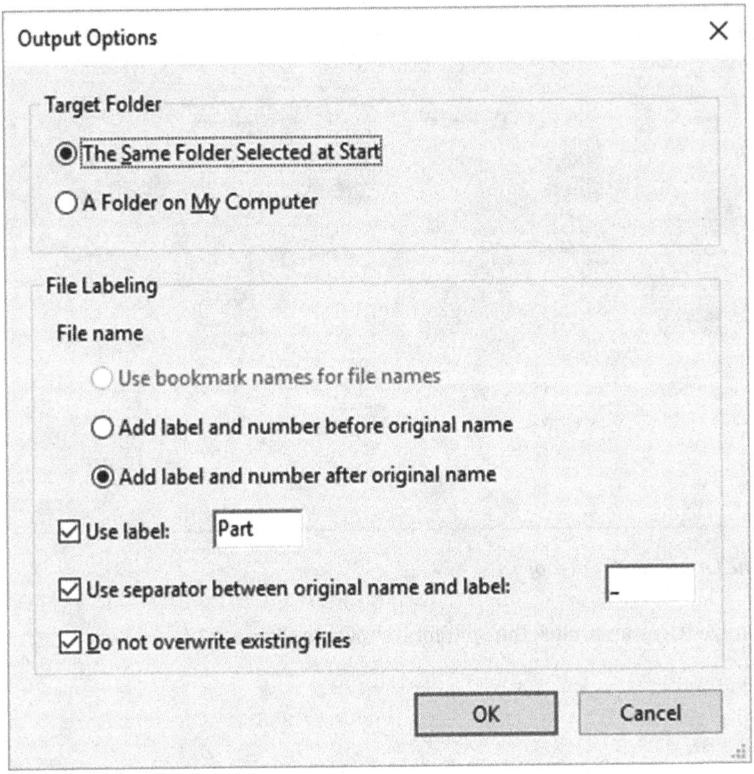

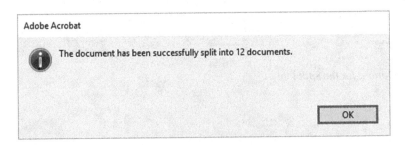

Figure 3-40. Output Options dialog box for the Split tool

Click OK if you made changes or click Cancel to simply exit if you made no changes.

Click the Split button. This will split each record so you will have 12 PDF files, one for each record. You will receive a notification like the one shown in Figure 3-41. Click OK.

Figure 3-41. Alert that the PDF document has been split

The original PDF file will still be intact. You can close it and exit Adobe Acrobat DC. However, in your file folder you will find 12 documents with endings of Part1 to Part12. You can rename these PDFs in your file folder or leave the names as is and e-mail the files to your clients.

Summary

In this chapter, you looked at how you could create single merge record documents for a presentation letter, whether it be a one-page or multipage letter. You used the Data Merge panel to add, preview, update, and remove a data source. Finally, you also looked at how to print, export, and separate pages in Adobe Acrobat DC Pro.

In the next chapter, you will look at how you can add images from a Data Merge.

■ **Note**   In my CSV file, I also have fields like e-mail and phone number, although these field values are fictitious. If you are sending the CSV to a printer outside of your company, remember that this information could be considered confidential and could be valuable to cyberthieves. A good tip to remember is if you are not planning to include the data in your merge, you should do one of three things:

- Delete it from your CSV first before you e-mail it to the print house.

- Print the document yourself on your printer in house.

- Only send a final PDF file that does not contain any extra information to your print house.

CHAPTER 4

Creating a Single Merge Record with Images Using the Data Merge Panel

Project: Creating a Product Sheet from Your CSV File

■ **Note** If you want to work along in this lesson or review the result, download your Chapter 4 files from http://www.apress.com/9781484231586. Work with the file with the label "Start." The file with the label "End" and the PDFs are the final result.

In the last chapter, you learned how to work with text in a data merge. However, in some cases if you are creating a product sheet of data or profile sheet for each of your top salespeople who will be at the convention, you need to be able to include images in your data merge. Let's look at how you can do that.

Open InDesign CC

To begin, open InDesign CC 2018. If you have not already set up your workspace, make sure to go back to Chapter 1 and review the information on creating a workspace for the Data Merge. Otherwise select the Data Merge Workspace or Reset Data Merge Workspace from the InDesign drop-down menu now, as shown in Figure 4-1.

© Jennifer Harder 2017
J. Harder, *Data Merge and Styles for Adobe InDesign CC 2018*,
https://doi.org/10.1007/978-1-4842-3159-3_4

Figure 4-1. The created Data Merge Workspace that you use to lay out a project

If you were beginning the files from scratch, you would choose File ➤ New Document and begin laying out the text and graphics that you might have created in Photoshop or Illustrator. However, for this chapter, choose File ➤ Open to open the document (Product_Start_1.indd) in the Chapter 4 folder, which is the file that contains the layout I have already created.

In this document, I have put the nonchanging elements in the Master Page A-Master in the Background layer and locked it, as displayed in Figures 4-2 and 4-3. I will put the Merge by itself on a layer named Data Merge. Although I could put this area in the Master area as well, I prefer to keep it outside on page 1 so I can easily access it.

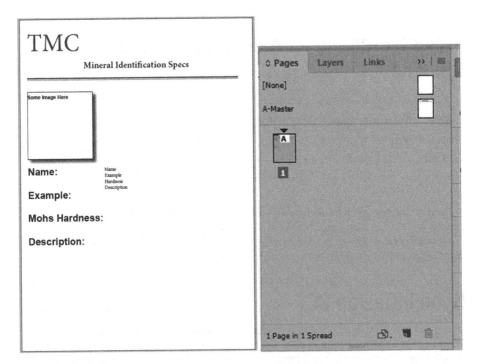

Figure 4-2. Thumbnail of the current page you will be working on. On page 1 some elements can be found in the Master Page A-Master

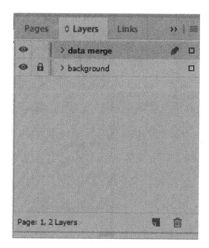

Figure 4-3. *The unchanging images and text are placed on the background layer and locked. The Data Merge elements are on their own layer on page 1 so you can easily access them while you edit the document*

Make sure that you start on page 1 and not on the Master Page. Refer to Figure 4-2.

Adding Paragraph Styles to the Data Merge

Click on the pasteboard area to ensure that none of the text is selected, then click Paragraph Styles in the docking station on the right to open the Paragraph Styles panel shown in Figure 4-4.

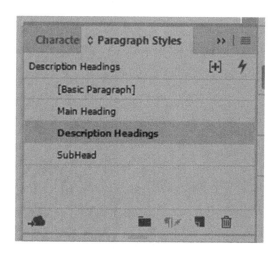

Figure 4-4. *The current styles are listed in the Paragraph Styles panel*

Notice that there are several paragraph styles already created for the document. However, when you highlight the text in the text box with the text tool, including the Name, Example, Hardness, and Description fields, this shows the default value of [Basic Paragraph], as shown in Figure 4-5.

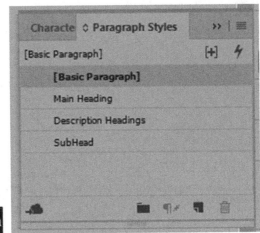

Figure 4-5. Currently the text that will be connected to the Data Merge is set to [Basic Paragraph] in the Paragraph Styles panel

Let's create a style for your Data Merge text that is based on the Description Headings style so that the text will line up evenly.

While the text is still highlighted, click the Create New Styles button highlighted in Figure 4-6.

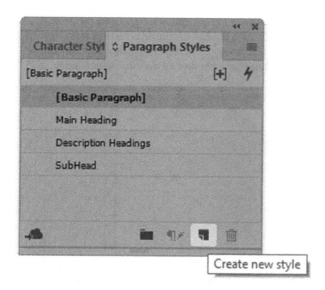

Figure 4-6. *While the text is still selected, click the Create New Style button*

Select the new Paragraph Style 1 that was just created, and shown in Figure 4-7, and double-click to open the Paragraph Style Options dialog box.

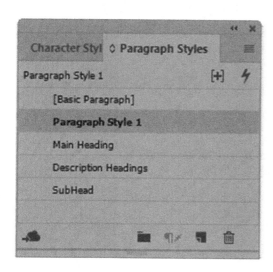

Figure 4-7. *The newly created style is highlighted and ready to rename*

On the General tab of the Paragraph Style Options dialog box, rename the new style Data Merge Styles, as shown in Figure 4-8. Also change the Based on setting from No Paragraph Style to Description Headings. This way the text will have the same spacing as the Description Heading style and you don't have to enter all the information again (see Figure 4-9).

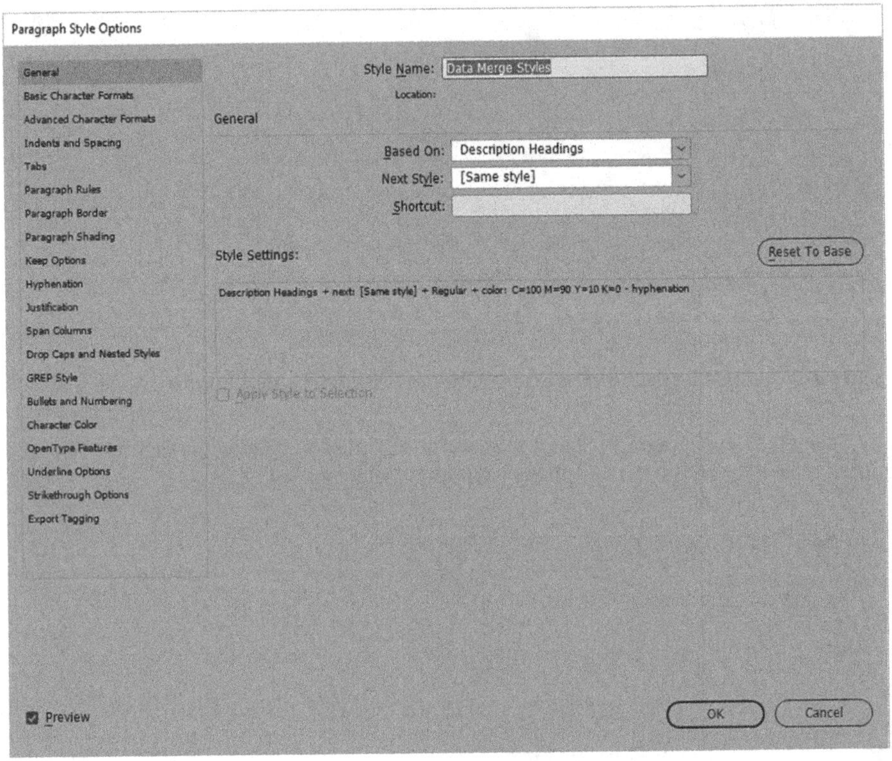

Figure 4-8. *The General tab of the Paragraph Style Options dialog box*

Name: Name

Example: Example

Mohs Hardness: Hardness

Description: Description

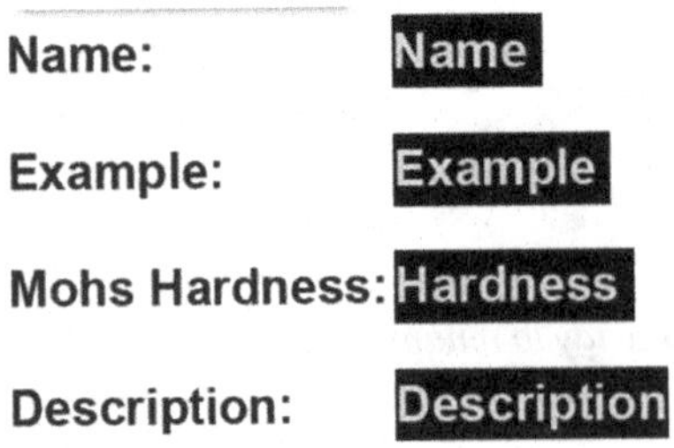

Figure 4-9. *Notice how the Merge text is now altered based on an earlier style*

For more details on the Paragraph Style Options General tab, review Chapter 2. You will now make a few changes on other tabs.

Click the Basic Character Formats tab. Change the Font Style to Regular, as depicted in Figure 4-10. For more details on the Basic Character Formats tab, review Chapter 2.

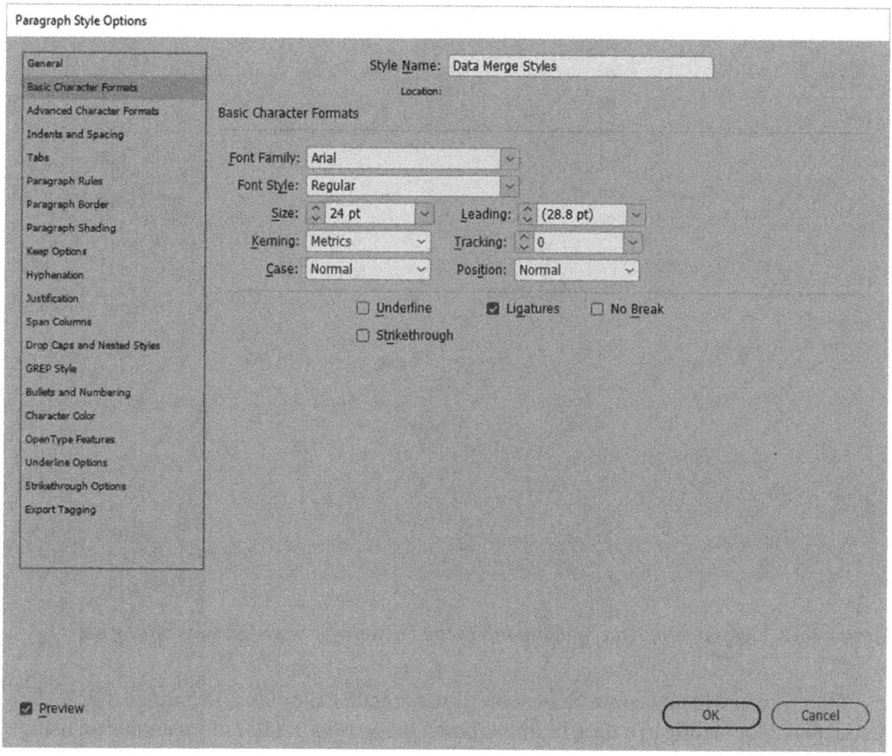

Figure 4-10. *The Basic Character Formats tab of the Paragraph Style Options dialog box*

On the Indents and Spacing tab, shown in Figure 4-11, settings have already been taken care of because you based the style on the Description Headings style, so you don't need to make any changes to the Space After setting because the baseline of both styles is now the same. For more details on using the Indents and Spacing tab, review Chapter 2.

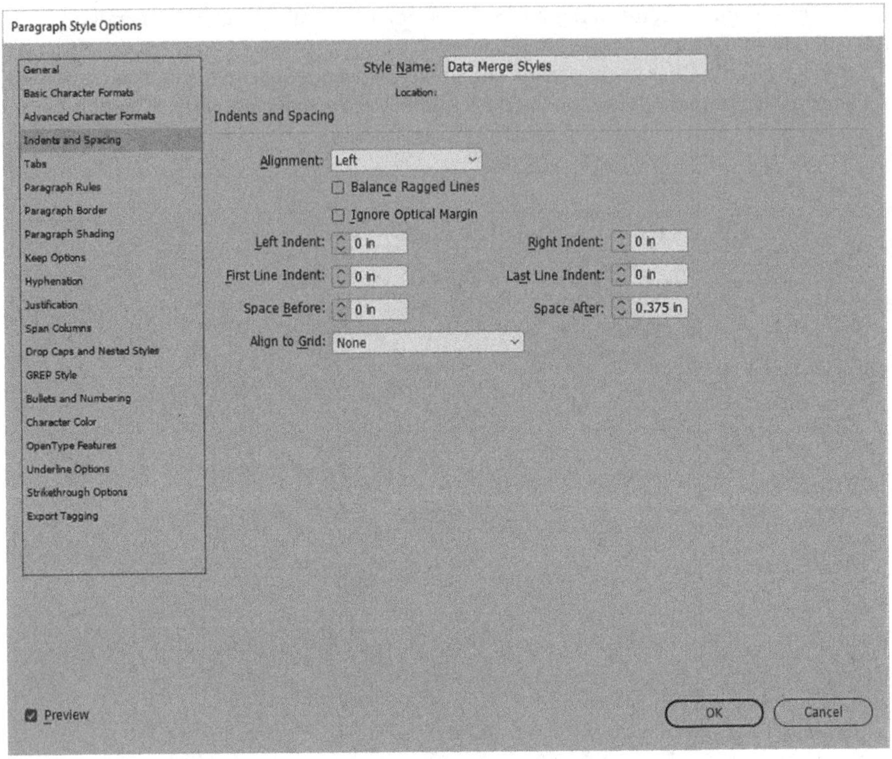

Figure 4-11. *The Indents and Spacing tab of the Paragraph Style Options dialog box*

Finally, you will make one change on the Character Color tab and change the Character Color setting to a dark blue, as shown in Figure 4-12. For more details on using the Character Color tab, review Chapter 2.

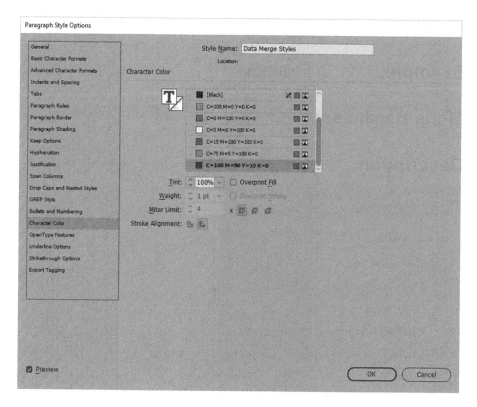

Figure 4-12. *The Character Color tab of the Paragraph Style Options dialog box*

When you are done, click OK to close the Paragraph Style Options dialog box. Your text should look like that shown in Figure 4-13.

Name: Name

Example: Example

Mohs Hardness: Hardness

Description: Description

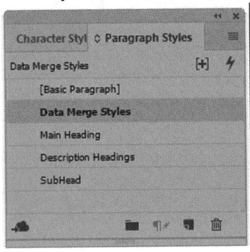

Figure 4-13. *The final text result after it is styled along with the newly created style in the Paragraph Styles panel*

Next you are going to create the Data Merge.

■ **Note**   If you do not know how to convert a Microsoft Excel file to a CSV (comma-delimited) file for InDesign, review Chapter 3.

Adding Image Fields in the Data Source File

Normally when you add an image to a page, you would draw a frame with a frame tool. While the frame is selected, go to File ➤ Place (or press Ctrl+D) to locate the image in a folder. Once you have selected the image you want to use, click Place, and the image will appear in the frame. This process is shown in Figure 4-14.

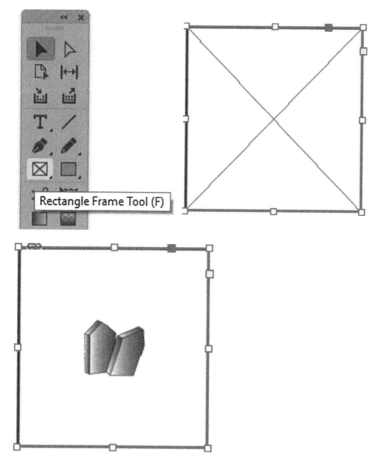

Figure 4-14. An image of some crystals appears inside of an image frame when placed

By adding image fields to the data source file, you can allow different images to appear on each merged record. For example, when you merge documents that include information from various companies, you can include an image of each company's logo, salesperson, or product as part of the merge. However, in this case the image is set in-line as part of the text rather than a separated graphic. Therefore, it must be included as part of a text box rather than a frame. As you can see in Figure 4-15, I have created two text boxes in my file: one that will house the image and another that will contain text.

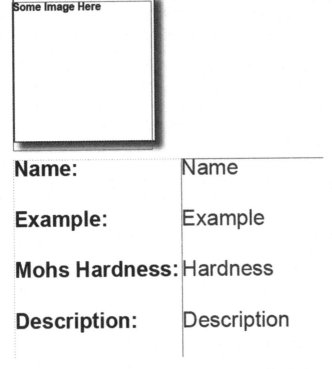

Figure 4-15. *The Data Merge image will appear in-line in the text box frame*

You can look at the Excel file mineral_list1 I created. Currently it has an area where you will need to add links for the photos.

At the beginning of the data field name, type an "at" symbol (@) to insert text or paths that refer to image files. The @ symbol is required only in the first line; subsequent lines should include the image paths. Paths, which are case-sensitive, must follow the naming conventions of the operating system in which they are stored.

If you get an error message when you type the @ symbol at the beginning of the field, type an apostrophe (') before the @ symbol (e.g., '@Photos) to validate the function. Some applications, such as Microsoft Excel, reserve the @ symbol for functions, so I would recommend you do this if you are starting with an Excel file or working in Excel on the file.

Tables 4-1 and 4-2 give examples of how you could add images depending on what format or folder they are in.

Table 4-1. *Example of Image References in Data Source File for Windows*

Name	Hardness	@Photos
Bladed	2	C:\Photos\cs_bladed.jpg
Dendritic	3	C:\MyDocuments\cs_dentritic.gif
Equant	6.5 to 7.5	C:\Photos\cs_equant.psd

Table 4-2. *Example of Image References in Data Source File for Mac OS*

Name	Hardness	@Photos
Bladed	2	Mac HD:Photos: cs_bladed.jpg
Dendritic	3	Desktop:Family: cs_dentritic.gif
Equant	6.5 to 7.5	Mac HD:Photos: cs_equant.psd

As you can see, InDesign can accept many image formats, including JPEG, GIF, Photoshop files, TIFFs, and so on. You must make sure that you write the correct link and file format.

In my example, you will find all the images for this project in the data_images folder and they are all JPEG files.

So, for example, you might type in Windows: C:\DataMergeProject\Chapter4\ Project3\data_images\cs_bladed.jpg. Add each correct name line under that in the @ Photos column.

After you are done typing the links, make sure to save the file as in Chapter 3 as a .csv file.

■ **Tip**   Window ➤ Links panel

You can use InDesign to view the path of an image on your operating system. Insert an image in an InDesign document, and then use the Links panel to view the image's location. With the image selected, select Copy Info ➤ Copy Full Path from the Links panel menu. You might need to edit the path after you paste it in your data source. This technique is especially useful for images on a server. Refer to Figure 4-16.

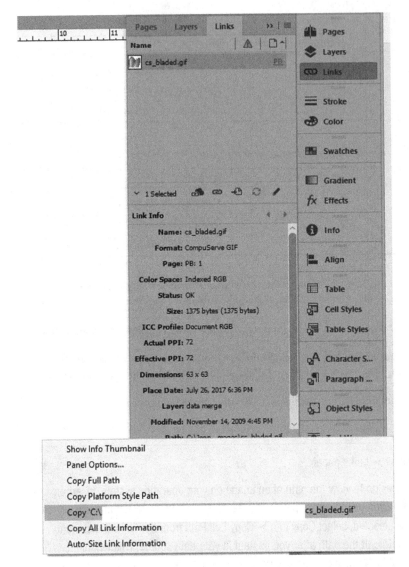

Figure 4-16. *You can temporarily place an image on a page if you need to copy the path link. This will speed up the process of typing if you have a number of images in that folder*

■ **Note** In Windows, you can also right-click on the link in your folder in File Explorer, select Copy Address and edit it in the .csv file.

After you have saved the `.csv` file with the new links, return to InDesign to start the Data Merge.

Starting the Data Merge

Go back to your Product_Start_1.indd file. In the Data Merge panel, select Select Data Source, as shown in Figure 4-17.

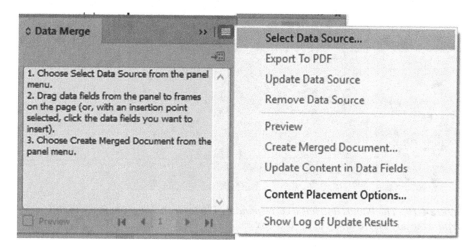

Figure 4-17. *In the Data Merge panel, select Select Data Source*

Locate the file mineral_list.csv and click Open, as shown in Figure 4-18.

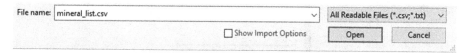

Figure 4-18. *Locate the .csv file for the Data Merge*

You will notice a new Photos icon, as shown in Figure 4-19.

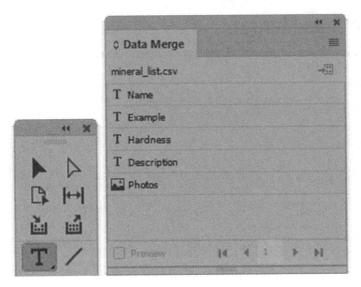

Figure 4-19. *The Photos link has a corresponding Photos icon. However, you will still require the text tool to link it in the text box*

With your Type tool, highlight the text where the photo should be, as depicted in Figure 4-20, and then in the Data Merge panel click the Photos icon.

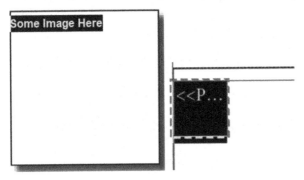

Figure 4-20. *The image Data Merge icon appears as a box in the Data Merge area when linked*

The icon will appear like Figure 4-21 in Normal mode, which shows the same viewing settings as used in Figure 4-20.

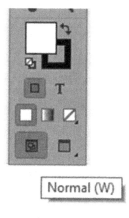

Figure 4-21. *View your document in Normal mode by clicking here in the Tools panel*

You can scale the photo frame by selecting it with the Selection tool (V) and dragging any one of its handles as shown in Figure 4-22.

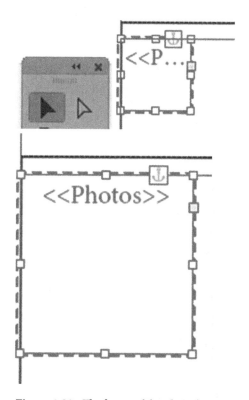

Figure 4-22. *The frame of the photo for Data Merge can be adjusted by dragging one of the handles while using the Selection tool*

147

Likewise, you can select the Image icon or text in the Data Merge panel and drag it into an empty frame as displayed in Figure 4-23.

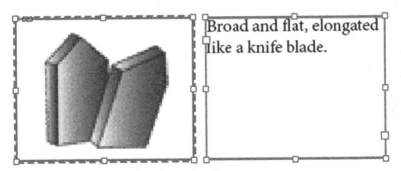

Figure 4-23. You can drag your Data Merge link into a frame if you don't want to highlight the text. This is how it appears in Preview mode

When the image is visible in Preview mode you can also adjust the display performance to check the resolution as shown in Figure 4-24. For now, leave this setting set to Typical Display.

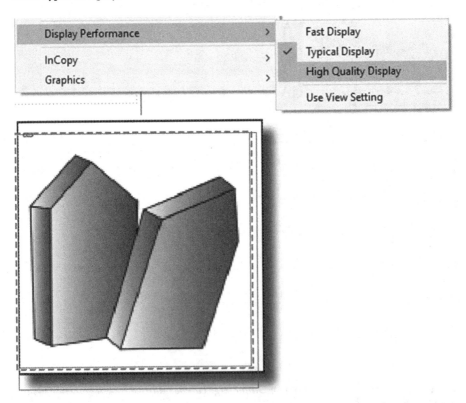

Figure 4-24. Viewing the image at the High Quality Display setting to check resolution

Select the Preview check box in the Data Merge panel to see if the image is appearing.

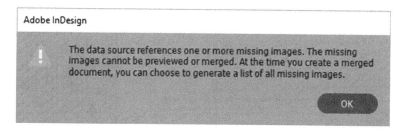

Note   For your own file, you might receive the alert shown in Figure 4-25 regarding a missing or incorrectly linked image.

Figure 4-25. You might see this alert if one or more images is not correctly linked

Make sure to go back into your Excel file and make any necessary corrections. Resave it as a `.csv` file and then close the file.

In InDesign, select Update Data Source, as shown in Figure 4-26.

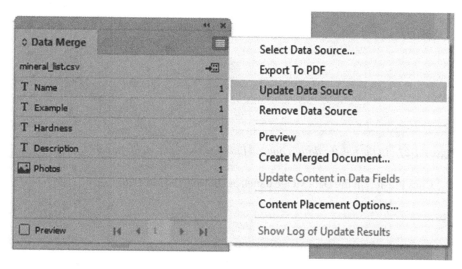

Figure 4-26. Always update the data source if you have made any changes to the .csv file to reflect the change in InDesign

Preview the file again and you should see the first image if everything is correctly linked.

Add the Data Merge to the other lines in the second text box by highlighting each of them and clicking that line in the Data Merge panel:

- Name

- Example

- Hardness

- Description

Your file should now look like Figure 4-27.

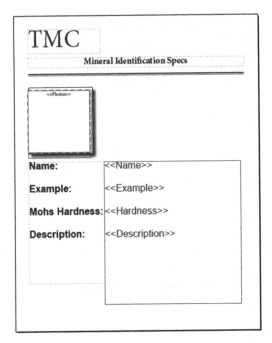

Figure 4-27. In the file, the data is now all linked to the Data Merge panel

Click Preview in the Data Merge panel, as shown in Figure 4-28.

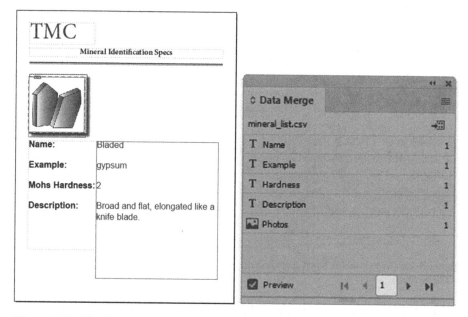

Figure 4-28. *The data appears on the first page of document, and you can preview each page using the Data Merge panel and its arrows*

Adjusting the Data Merge Text

After you have previewed each page using the arrows, you might notice that some of the text in the description area is hyphenated, as displayed in Figure 4-29. You might not want this to occur in your text.

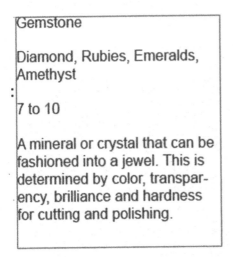

Figure 4-29. Note how the word transparancy is hyphenated due to its length and the size of the text box

To change this hyphenation setting, click with your Selection tool somewhere on the pasteboard. With no text selected, double-click Data Merge Styles in the Paragraph Styles panel, shown in Figure 4-30, to open the the Paragraph Style Options dialog box.

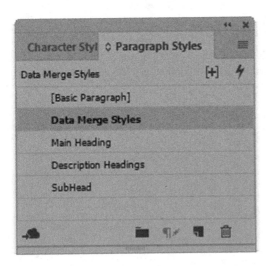

Figure 4-30. Double-click Data Merge Styles in the Paragraph Styles panel

The Hyphenation Tab

On the Hyphenation tab of the Paragraph Style Options dialog box, shown in Figure 4-31, clear the Hyphenate check box (see Figure 4-32).

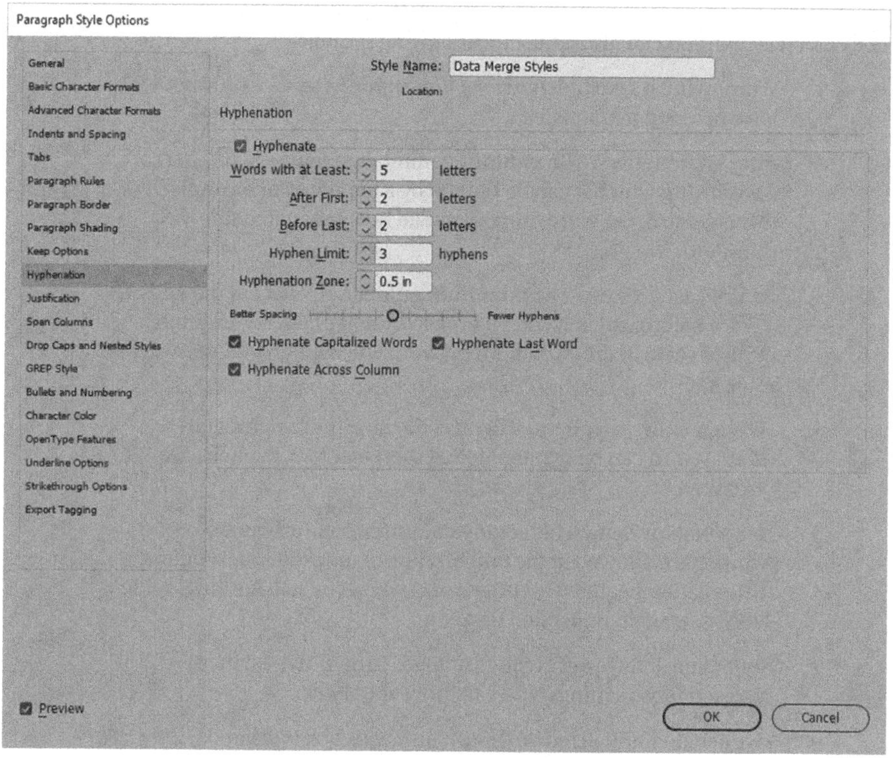

Figure 4-31. *The Hyphenation tab of the Paragraph Style Options dialog box*

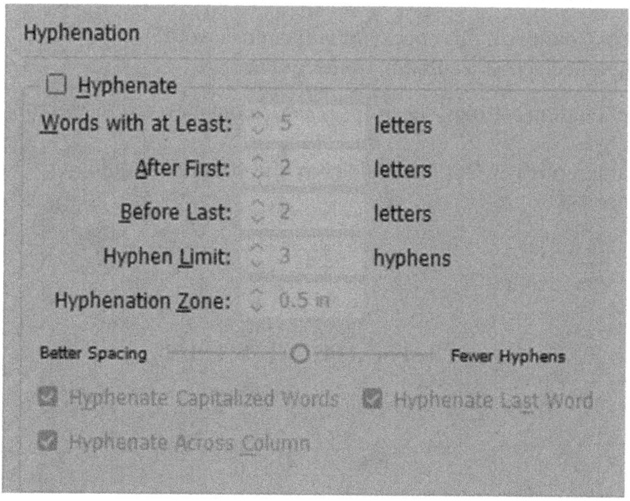

Figure 4-32. *Clear the Hyphenate check box on the Hyphenation tab of the Paragraph Style Options dialog box*

We have not yet explored the Hyphenate tab. If you want to leave the Hyphenate check box selected, you can also adjust the following settings.

- Words with at Least _ letters: Set how many letters a word should have before it hyphenates.

- After First _ letters: The minimum number of letters at the start of a word after which it can be broken by a hyphen. For example, if this is set to 3, the word mineral would be hyphenated this way: min-eral.

- Before Last _ letters: The minimum number of letters at the end of a word before which it can be broken by a hyphen. For example, if this is set to 3, the word mineral would be hyphenated this way: mine-ral.

- Hyphen Limit _ hyphens: This sets the maximum number of times a word can be hyphenated. If this is set to 0, hyphens are unlimited.

- Hyphenation Zone: This setting determines the amount of white space allowed at the end of a line of unjustified text before hyphenation begins. This only works when you use the Single-line Composer with unjustified text.

- Better Spacing–Fewer Hyphens range: To alter the balance between these settings, you can move the slider.

- Hyphenate Capitalized Words: If this check box is cleared, capitalized words will not be hyphenated.

- Hyphenate Last Word: If this check box is cleared, the last word in a paragraph will not be hyphenated.

- Hyphenate Across Column: If this check box is cleared, a word will not be hyphenated across a column, frame, or page.

For more details on hyphenation settings, see `https://helpx.adobe.com/indesign/using/text-composition.html`.

Click OK to close the Paragraph Style Options dialog box and your text should not hyphenate, as shown in Figure 4-33.

Gemstone

Diamond, Rubies, Emeralds,
Amethyst

7 to 10

A mineral or crystal that can
be fashioned into a jewel.
This is determined by color,
transparency, brilliance and
hardness for cutting and
polishing.

Figure 4-33. The paragraph is now shown with the hyphenation adjusted

As you can see, Data Merge and Paragraph styles can work together. Any change to any tab of the Paragraph Style Options dialog box will affect the text that is displayed in the Data Merge.

Content Placement Options

In the Data Merge panel, in the drop-down menu, select Content Placement Options, as shown in Figure 4-34. This opens the Content Placement Options dialog box shown in Figure 4-35.

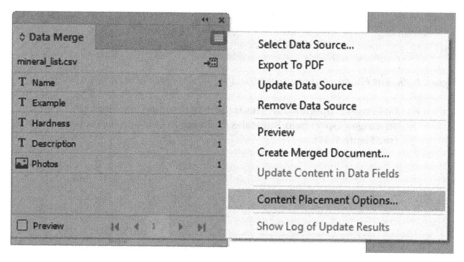

Figure 4-34. In the Data Merge panel, select Content Placement Options

Content Placement Options

Image Placement

Fitting: Fit Images to Frames

☐ Center In Frame

☑ Link Images

☐ Remove Blank Lines for Empty Fields

☐ Record Limit per Document: 50

OK

Reset

Figure 4-35. *The Content Placement Options dialog box*

The following options appear in the Content Placement Options dialog box (Figure 4-36):

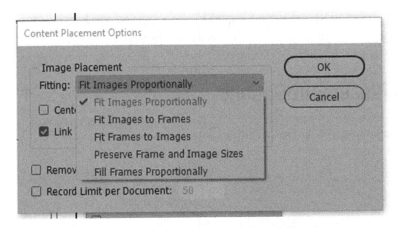

Figure 4-36. *The Fitting drop-down menu in the Content Placement Options dialog box*

- Fit Images Proportionally: This is the default setting. It maintains an image's aspect ratio, but scales the image to fit within the frame (see Figure 4-37).

Figure 4-37. *The crystal image shown using the Fit Images Proportionally setting*

- Fit Images to Frames: The image is scaled so that its aspect ratio is the same as the frame (see Figure 4-38).

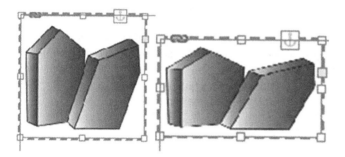

Figure 4-38. *The crystal image shown using the Fit Images to Frames setting*

- Fit Frames to Images: The image size is maintained, but the frame size is adjusted to match it. The frame could shrink or grow, depending on the image size (see Figure 4-39).

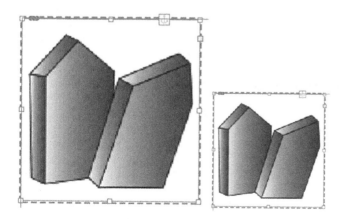

Figure 4-39. *The crystal image shown using the Fit Frames to Images setting*

157

- Preserve Frame and Image Sizes: The image is placed at its current size in the frame. If it is too large, it will be cropped by the frame (see Figure 4-40).

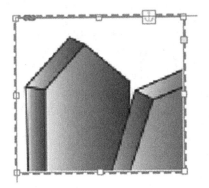

Figure 4-40. *The crystal image shown using the Preserve Frame and Image Sizes setting*

- Fill Frames Proportionally: The image's width or height fills the frame. If any area is larger, it is cropped (see Figure 4-41).

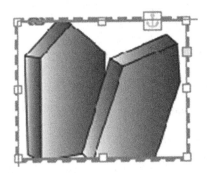

Figure 4-41. *The crystal image shown using the Fill Frames Proportionally setting*

- Center in Frame: The center of the image and frame are aligned (see Figure 4-42).

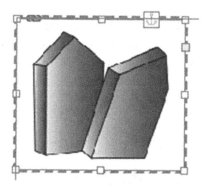

Figure 4-42. *The crystal image shown using the Center in Frame setting*

- Link Images: When selected, this setting creates a link or file path to the current image. If this check box is cleared, the image data will be embedded in the InDesign document.

- Remove Blank Lines for Empty Fields: When selected, this setting removes paragraph returns that are inserted for empty fields. This is often used for mailing with optional address fields. It ignores soft returns. If there are any characters or spaces on a line, that line is not deleted.

- Record Limit per Document: This setting assigns the maximum number of records for a merged document. When this limit is reached, a new document is created to hold the remaining records. You can only use this option when Single Records is selected on the Records tab.

- Page Limit per Document: This setting determines the maximum number of pages for each document. When this limit is reached, a new document is created to hold the remaining pages. You can only use this option when Multiple Records is selected on the Records tab.

    Note: because we are using a single record in this project you will not see this option in the current dialog box.

Leave the Fitting setting at Fit Images Proportionally and leave the Center in Frame check box cleared. When done, click OK to close the Content Placement Options dialog box.

■ **Note**   If you try to change these options and click OK while you are in Preview mode in the Data Merge panel, you will see the warning shown in Figure 4-43. Click OK and clear the Preview check box, and then check Preview mode again to see the change.

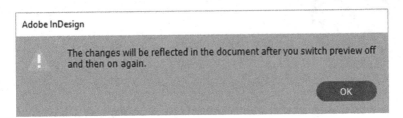

Figure 4-43. *Warning that you need to switch Preview off and on before you'll see the update result*

Any change that you make to the size of one image in the Data Merge affects the display of them all. Therefore, when you are sizing your photos in Adobe Photoshop, make sure that they all have the same size (e.g., 3 inches by 4 inches) before you link them. Any image that is a slightly different proportion could result in unwanted display results, such as a cropped or a fuzzy image. Be consistent with your layout when using images in the Data Merge.

Creating the Merged Document and Exporting as a PDF

On the Data Merge panel, select Export to PDF, as shown in Figure 4-44.

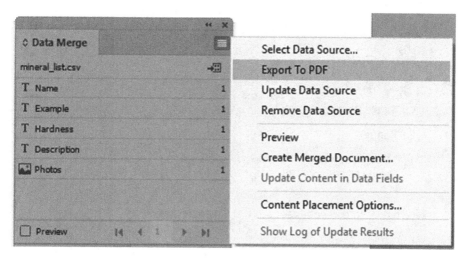

Figure 4-44. *Exporting the merged document as a PDF*

In the Create Merged Document dialog box adjust the following areas on the Records tab (see Figure 4-45) and Options tab (see Figure 4-46).

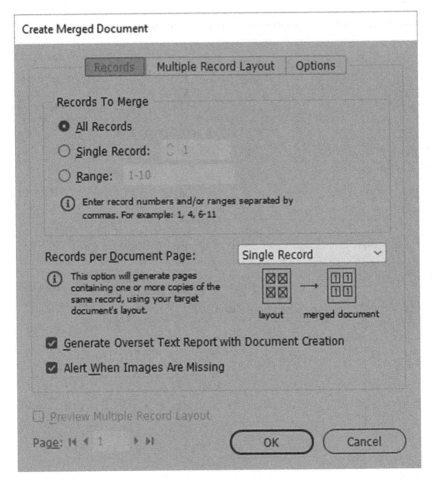

Figure 4-45. The Records tab of the Create Merged Document dialog box

Skip the Multiple Record Layout tab and click the Options tab shown in Figure 4-46.

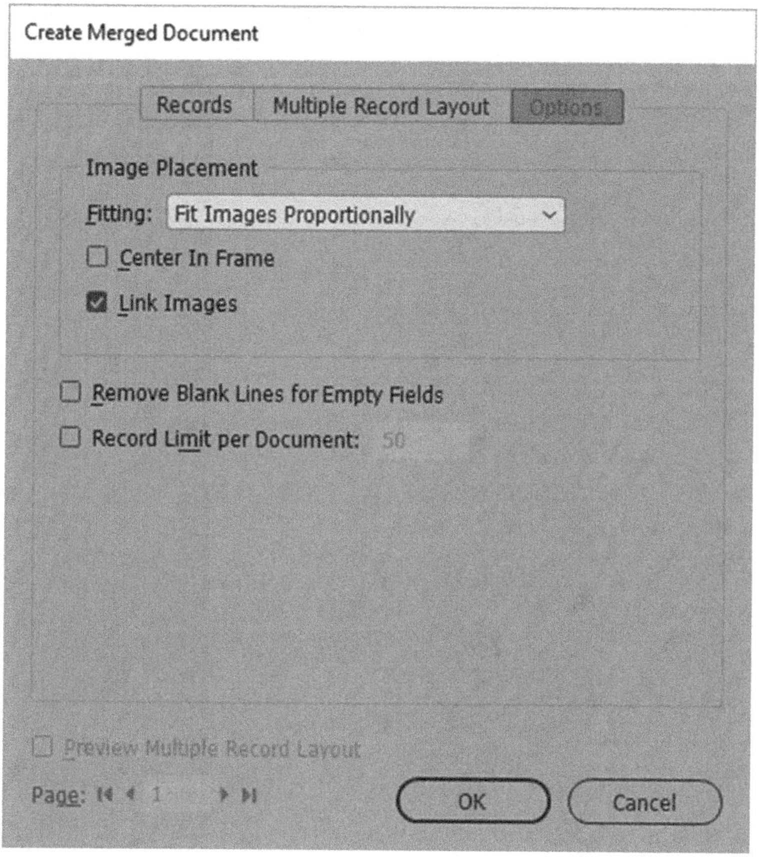

Figure 4-46. *The Options tab of the Create Merged Document dialog box*

Notice that this area is basically the same as the Content Placement Options dialog box. If at the last minute you want to make further adjustments, you could do it here. It also retains whatever changes were made in the Content Placement Options dialog box.

Click OK to open the Export Adobe PDF dialog box, shown in Figure 4-47. Refer to Chapter 3 if you need to review this dialog box's functions.

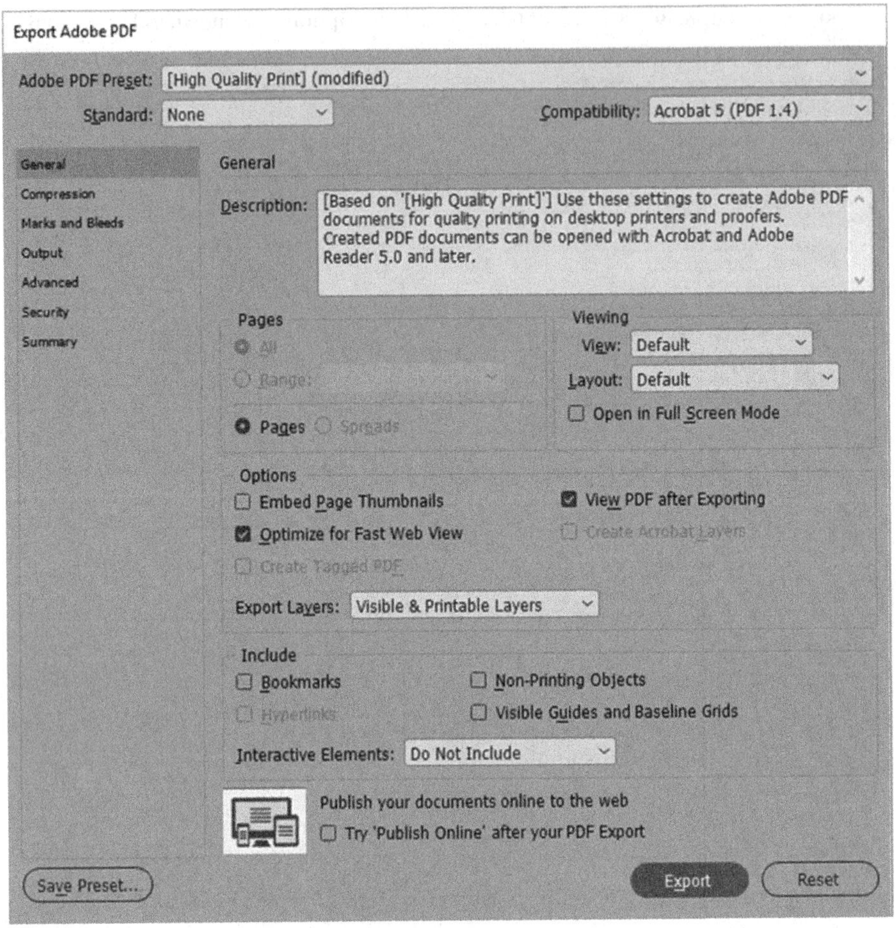

Figure 4-47. The Export Adobe PDF dialog box

Click Export. Next, save the files in the desired location as Product_End_1a.pdf as shown in Figure 4-48. Click Save.

Figure 4-48. Save the document as a PDF

■ **Note**   You might get an alert like the one shown in Figure 4-49 indicating that no overset text was created. Click OK.

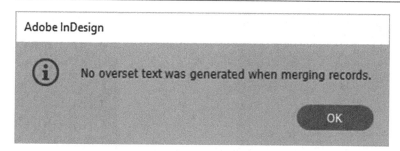

Figure 4-49. *Alert that appears if no overset text was generated*

The file will open in Adobe Acrobat DC for you to view. Make sure to go back and save your InDesign file with the Preview cleared in the Data Merge panel. Otherwise you will see the alert shown in Figure 4-50. Click OK and follow the instructions.

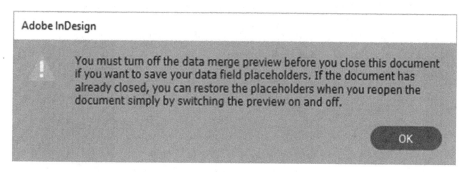

Figure 4-50. *Alert that appears if you try to close the document while the Preview is still on in the Data Merge panel*

Can I Use Object, Table, and Cell Styles as Part of My Data Merge?

Currently only Paragraph and Character styles can be used in Data Merge text. However, you can apply Object styles to a frame or table that could be on the Template layer, as I did in my example. I placed a drop shadow around my frame and saved it in the Window ➤ Styles ➤ Object Styles panel, as shown in Figure 4-51. In the Object Style Options dialog box, shown in Figure 4-52, just make sure that the text boxes for your Data Merge are transparent and cover an area within your frame or table. When you create your merged PDF, if done correctly it will look as though the image is within the object frame or table.

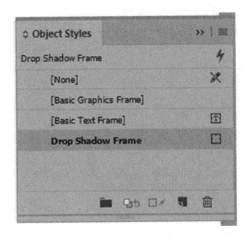

Figure 4-51. *Adding Object styles to the Object Styles panel*

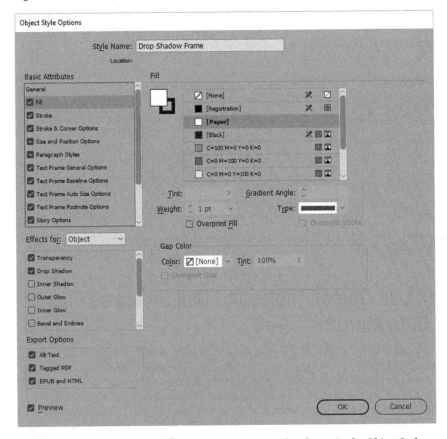

Figure 4-52. *There are many choices you can use to style a frame in the Object Style Options dialog box*

For a tables, you can create a text box, and then, while your cursor is inside the menu, choose Table ➤ Insert Table.

To insert a data fields into grouped items, table cells, or nested boxes, drag the image field onto the target. Refer here to Figure 4-53.

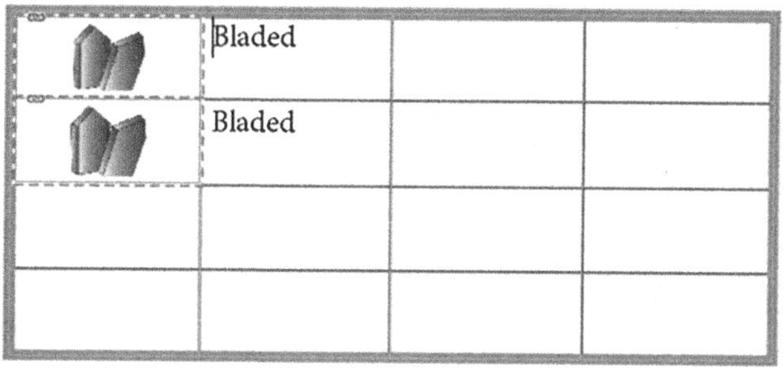

Figure 4-53. *Data Merge fields were added to a table. Here it is being viewed in Preview mode*

Tables and cells can be useful if, let's say, you must include more than one image on a page. For example, perhaps a salesperson has several awards or logos that need to be displayed with his or her name.

Earlier in your mineral list .csv file, you created a column heading called '@Photos. You can create second column heading called '@Photos2. In this column, you can create a new list of links and select this new data source.

Figure 4-54 shows what that looks like in the Data Merge panel and in the table cells. See the file Table_Example_2Photos.indd.

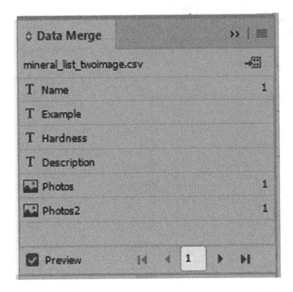

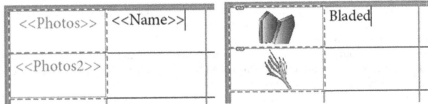

Figure 4-54. *The Data Merge panel when two columns of photos are added and how it appears in a table with Preview mode off and on*

You can also create a second column of names for this second set of pictures. You will be doing that with numbers in Chapter 5.

Adding a QR Code in the Date Merge

You can also add QR codes either as graphics or as text with the `.csv` file.

- Plain Text: Type this as you would any other text. Example: Hello Friend

- Web Hyperlink: Example: URL: `http://www.google.com`

- Text Message: Example: SMSTO:9818143575:Hello

- Email: Example: MATMSG:TO:johnsmith@tmc.com;SUB:Hi;BODY:;;;

- Business Card: Example: BEGIN:VCARD\nVERSION:2.1\
nN:Smith;Sue\nFN:Sue Smith\nORG:Tourmaline Mining
Corporation\nTITLE:Engineer\nTEL;CELL:+919876543289\
nTEL;WORK;VOICE:123456789\nADR;WORK:;;Street
ABC;Vancouver;BC;V5K4RQ;Canada\nEMAIL;WORK;
INTERNET:sue@tmc.com\nURL: www.mywebsite.com\
nEND:VCARD

Look at my e-mail example in file QRCode_Example.indd and refer to Figures 4-55
and 4-56.

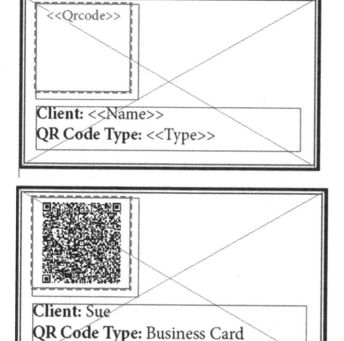

Figure 4-55. *How a QR code would appear on a business card if the link is from a .csv file
linked via the Data Merge panel With Preview mode off and on*

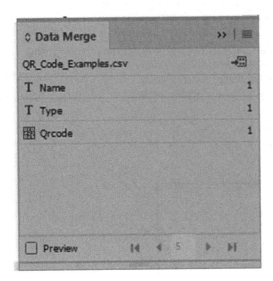

Figure 4-56. The Data Merge panel with a Qrcode link icon

To create a column for the QR code, I named the heading of the column #Qrcode. You must always use a pound sign (#) before the heading. This tells the Data Merge to generate a QR code in the same way as using Menu Object ➤ Generate a QR Code.

QR codes act like images in the Data Merge panel and you can adjust their content placement options as you would for any other image.

For an overview on Data Merge and QR code formats you can also view https://helpx.adobe.com/indesign/using/data-merge.html.

The blog post at https://indesignsecrets.com/data-merge-qr-codes-explained.php also gives a nice overview on how to use QR codes on business cards for e-mails.

Summary

In this chapter, you explored how to add images and QR codes to your InDesign files via the Data Merge panel. You also discovered that Paragraph styles can be use be used to alter the appearance of text that is part of Data Merge. Finally, like any other PDF file, these files can be exported as PDFs to Adobe Acrobat DC Pro.

In the next chapter, you are going to look at how to create multiple merge records using the Data Merge panel.

Creating a Multiple Merge Record Using the Data Merge Panel

Project: Creating a Raffle Ticket Layout for Print, Part 2

Note   If you want to work along in this lesson or review the result, download your Chapter 5 files from http://www.apress.com/9781484231586. Work with the file with the label "Start." The file with the label "End" and the PDFs are the final result.

For the last several chapters we have looked at merging single records. Now we will look at multiple merge records. Much of what we have learned in the earlier lessons can be applied to multiple merges when it comes to setting up your .csv files. However, the layout for the file in Adobe InDesign CC is a bit more challenging.

Open InDesign CC

To begin, open InDesign CC 2018. If you have not already set up your workspace, make sure to go back to Chapter 1 and review the information on creating a workspace for the Data Merge. Otherwise, select the Data Merge Workspace or Reset Data Merge Workspace from the InDesign drop-down menu, as shown in Figure 5-1.

© Jennifer Harder 2017
J. Harder, *Data Merge and Styles for Adobe InDesign CC 2018*,
https://doi.org/10.1007/978-1-4842-3159-3_5

Figure 5-1. *The Data Merge Workspace that you use for all your projects in this chapter*

If you were beginning the files from scratch, you would choose File ➤ New Document and begin laying out the text and graphics that you might have created in Photoshop or Illustrator. However, for this chapter, choose File ➤ Open to open the document (Raffle_10upMerge_start.indd) in the Chapter 5 folder, which is the file that contains the layout I have already created.

The Data Merge Panel

The final thing you can do with Data Merge is create a multiple merge (see Figure 5-2). This is like working with labels in Microsoft Word.

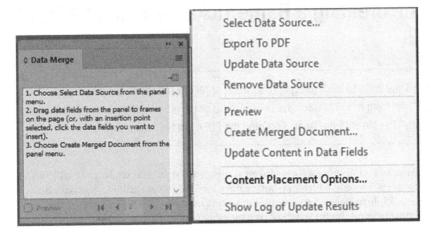

Figure 5-2. *The Data Merge Workspace panel also allows you to create multiple merges*

Multiple merges can sometimes be tricky in regard to text placement, but otherwise they are the same as single records. Use only one Master Page if you are planning on doing a multiple merge. Only work with one page in a multiple merge, as more than one page will confuse the program. If you have pages that are not part of the merge, keep them separate and combine them at the print stage or in Adobe Acrobat DC Pro as a PDF later.

Creating Double Custom Numbering for Your CSV File

You'll use the same Employee_List_2.csv file as you did in the previous lesson.

If you do not know how to convert your Microsoft Excel file to a .csv file, review Chapter 3.

The .csv file you are using has custom numbering, Employee Number, that was typed into an Excel file. That file was then converted to a .csv file. If you would prefer to use sequential numbering, read the section "Final Thoughts and Using Sequential Numbering" later in this chapter.

As in Figure 5-3, make sure to select your data source and set the text that will be part of the merge in your InDesign document.

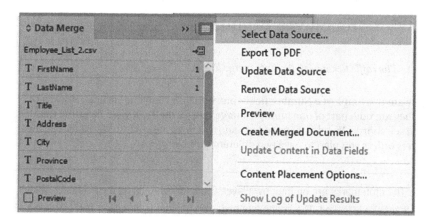

Figure 5-3. *Select Select Data Source from the Data Merge panel menu*

This time you'll work on another raffle ticket file that uses employee names and numbers instead, with a rip-away area, as shown in Figure 5-4.

Tourmaline Mining Corporation
Raffle Draw
May 8-9
Keep your Ticket
If we call your number, you have won a
fantastic prize!

<<FirstName>> <<LastName>>
Number: <<Employee Number>>

<<Employee Number>>

Figure 5-4. *The raffle ticket with the date merge layout*

There are two Employee Number fields, one horizonal and one vertical. However, because they are both part of one multiple merge record, they will yield the same number, as you will see shortly. You do not need to create two separate columns in your .csv file for numbers unless you plan to have two different number types.

■ **Note** The crop marks are on their own layer, Cropmarks, again on the A-Master Master Page and that layer is locked. The image and text is on another layer called Text on page 1 (see Figure 5-5).

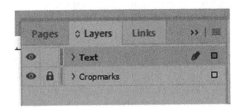

Figure 5-5. *The two layers in the current open document. Currently you are working on the Text layer*

Also in the Paragraph Styles panel, I have applied two styles, one to horizontal black text and another to the vertical white text on the red background, as shown in Figure 5-6. The white style is based on the black style; only the color is different. Review Chapter 4 if you are not sure how to create this setting.

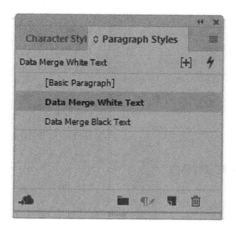

Figure 5-6. *Two styles have been created for the text: one is for white text and the other is for black text*

On the Text layer, using the Selection tool (V), select all the items and select Object ➤ Group or press Ctrl+G or Command+G.

Group the items you want to have part as of the merge as one unit and do not leave them as separate items. You will know that they are a group because a dotted line will run around the group when it is selected, as shown in Figure 5-7.

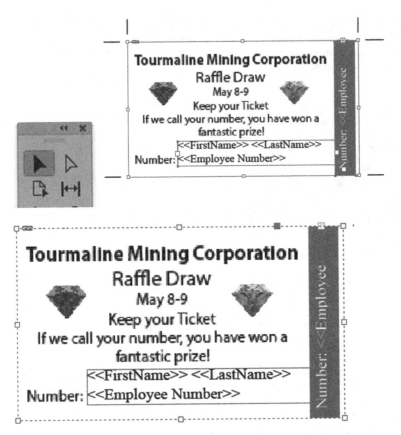

Figure 5-7. *With the Selection tool, all the items on the text layer have been grouped so that that they will move as one unit during the multiple data merge*

■ **Note** Do not be concerned if you see an error message at the bottom left of your InDesign console, as shown in Figure 5-8. This is referring to overset text, which will not show up once you preview the merge. Sometimes the column heading from the .csv file is longer than the actual content or text box, so when Preview is not selected in the Data Merge panel you might see this error, but you can ignore it for now.

Figure 5-8. *An error message displayed at the bottom of the document console. You can ignore this error for now because you are not in the Data Merge panel Preview mode*

Working with the Layers and Pages Panels (Review)

As mentioned earlier, you only need one item on the page. If you have crop marks they need to be on your Master Page so they don't move with the rest of the multiple merge and make sure to lock this layer. Remember, anything you don't want to move must be on your Master Page in a separate layer and locked. In my case it is on A-Master, as displayed in Figure 5-9.

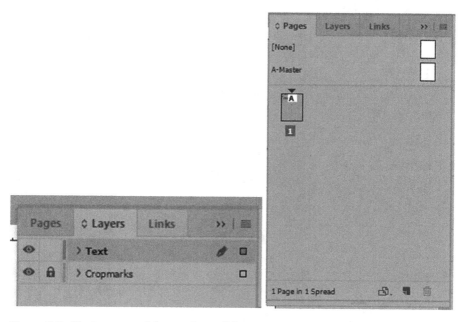

Figure 5-9. *The images and the text that will be merged should now all be grouped on the Text layer and on Page 1*

As you saw earlier, I put my grouped merge on its own layer called Text.

Creating a Multiple Merge Record Layout

Preview the merge using the arrow icons at the bottom of the Data Merge panel, shown in Figure 5-10, to check for overset. If there is none, continue with the lesson.

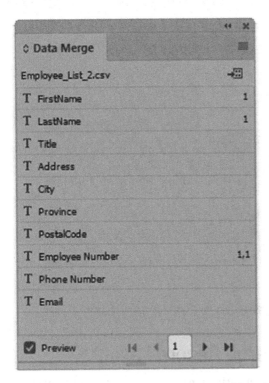

Figure 5-10. Preview the Data Merge to see if there is any overset text

Next, select Create Merged Document from the Data Merge panel shortcut menu, shown in Figure 5-11.

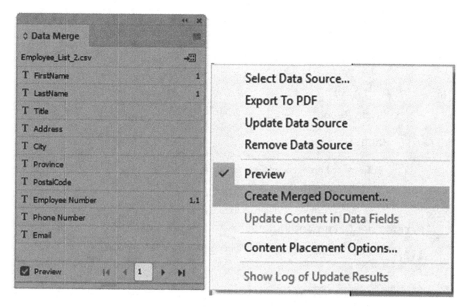

Figure 5-11. *Start creating the multiple merge by selecting Create Merged Document from the Data Merge panel shortcut menu*

On the Records tab of the Create Merged Document dialog box, shown in Figure 5-12, for the Records per Document Page drop-down list, select Multiple Records.

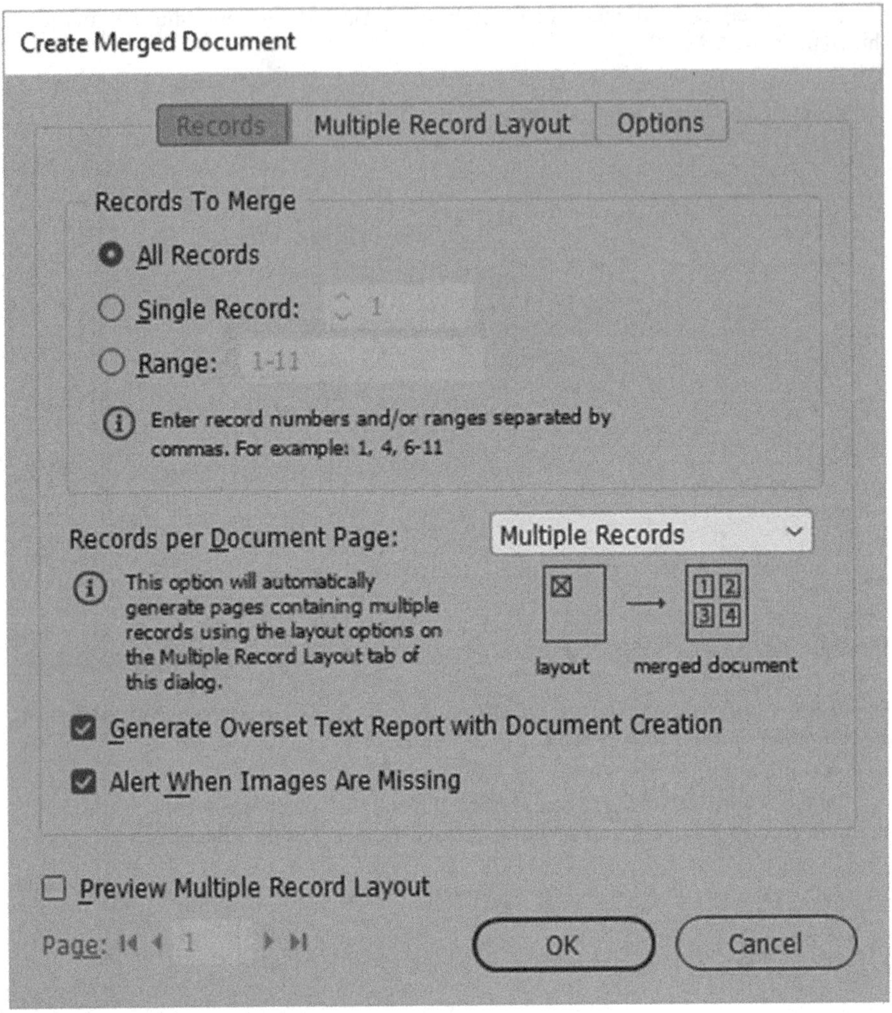

Create Merged Document

| Records | Multiple Record Layout | Options |

Records To Merge

◉ All Records

○ Single Record: ○ 1

○ Range: 1-11

(i) Enter record numbers and/or ranges separated by
commas. For example: 1, 4, 6-11

Records per Document Page: | Multiple Records ⌄ |

(i) This option will automatically
generate pages containing multiple
records using the layout options on
the Multiple Record Layout tab of
this dialog.

layout → merged document

☑ Generate Overset Text Report with Document Creation

☑ Alert When Images Are Missing

☐ Preview Multiple Record Layout

Page: ⏮ ◀ 1 ▶ ⏭   (OK)   (Cancel)

☑ Preview Multiple Record Layout

Page: ⏮ ◀ 1 ▶ ⏭

Figure 5-12. The Records tab of the Create Merged Records dialog box

Also select the Preview Multiple Record Layout check box.

You can use the arrows for the Page field to move through the record layout and see how many multiple records appear on one page. However, you will only be able to view one page of records, not the entire document.

On the Multiple Record Layout tab, shown in Figure 5-13, adjust the following settings.

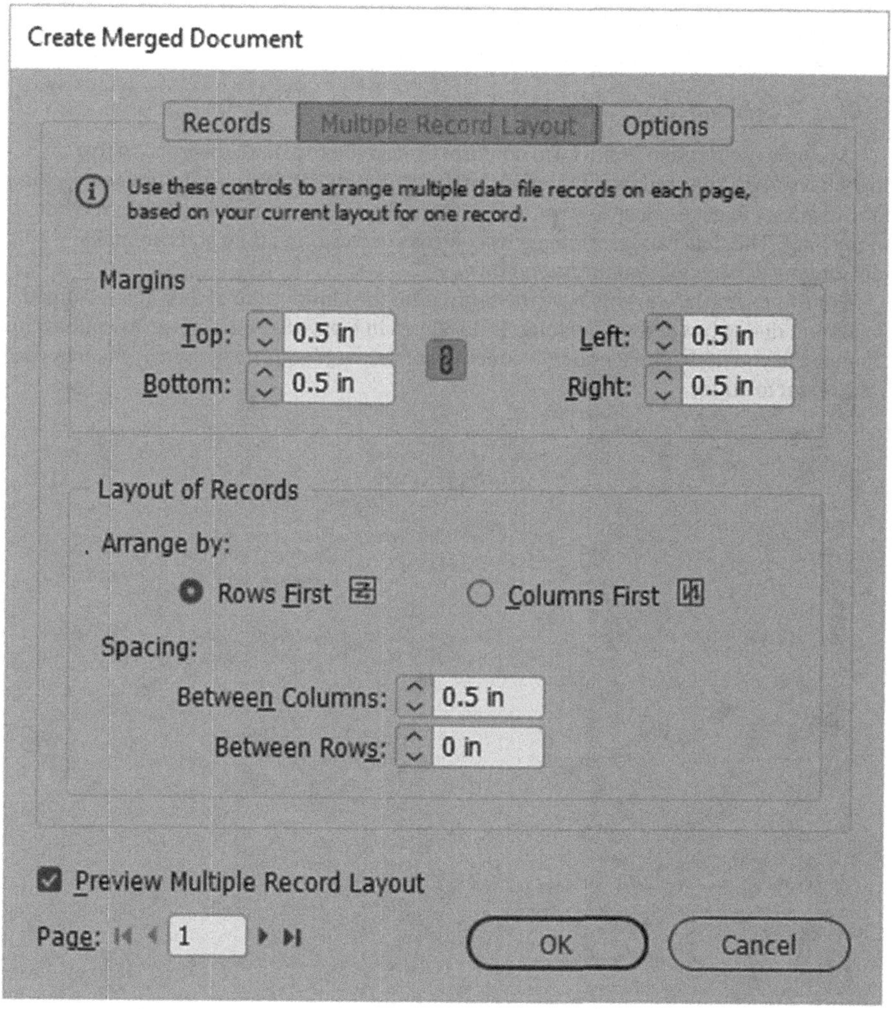

Figure 5-13. *The Multiple Record Layout tab of the Create Merged Records dialog box*

In the Margins section, click the Link icon. You can unlink the margins for your own custom layout. The settings for Top, Bottom, Left, and Right margins should all be set to 0.5 inches.

In the Layout of Records section, there are two Arrange By options:

- Rows First: This option will move the data left to right.

- Columns First: This option will move the data up and down.

Also in the Layout of Records section, there are two settings for Spacing.

- Between Columns: This is set to 0.5 inches.

- Between Rows: This is set to 0 inches.

Multiple records can be tricky to conform exactly to crop mark margins, so this might have to be adjusted later in the final merged document. Watch your preview as you adjust, and try to get as close as you can with your file so you get the desired ten records on the page. The data can be arranged by columns or rows, and then you can make adjustments between the columns and rows.

For this example, you will leave the settings on the Options tab of the Create Merged Document dialog box at their defaults, as displayed in Figure 5-14. However, as you saw in Chapter 4, if you added images or QR codes to your Data Merge, this might be an area you would want to adjust.

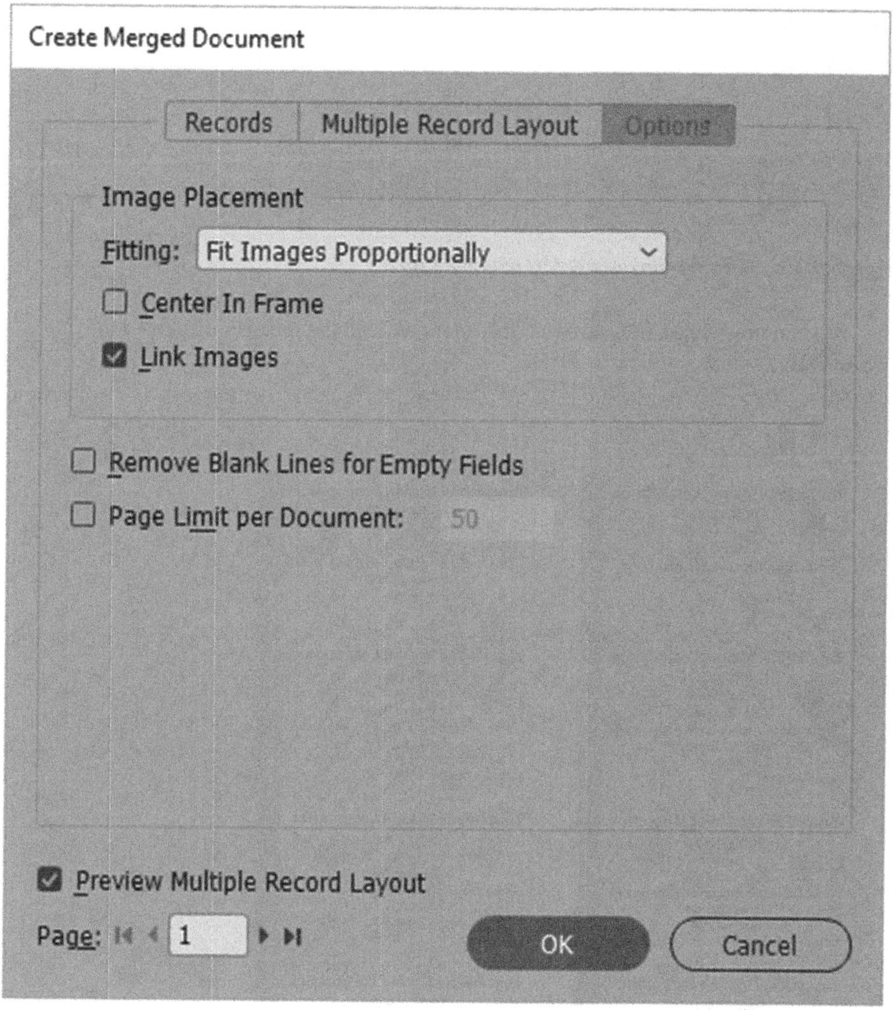

Create Merged Document

| Records | Multiple Record Layout | Options |

Image Placement

Fitting: Fit Images Proportionally ⌄

☐ Center In Frame

☑ Link Images

☐ Remove Blank Lines for Empty Fields

☐ Page Limit per Document: 50

☑ Preview Multiple Record Layout

Page: ⏮ ◀ 1 ▶ ⏭   OK   Cancel

Figure 5-14. The Options tab of the Create Merged Records dialog box

When done, click OK. Give InDesign time to generate the new file. If everything is okay, you will get a message indicating that no overset text was generated, as shown in Figure 5-15.

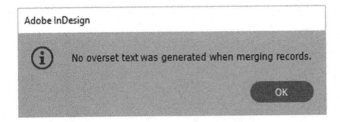

Figure 5-15. *Alert that no overset text was generated*

You can now view a new merged document with all the records, displayed in Figure 5-16.

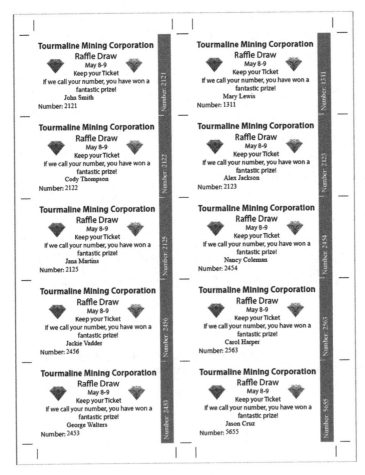

Figure 5-16. *Page 1 of your generated merged record*

In my case, because I had 12 names, two names went onto the next page as this is a ten-up layout. The rest of the page was blank except for the crop marks on the Master Page, as shown in Figure 5-17.

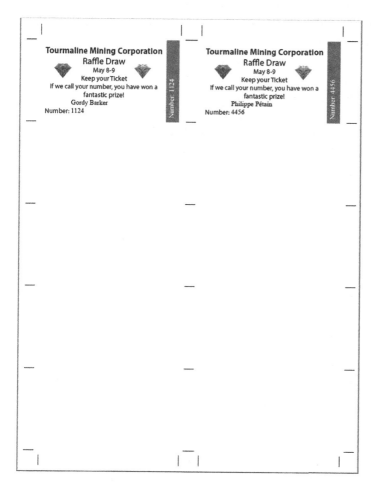

Figure 5-17. *Page 2 of your generated merged record. There are only two records on this page and the rest is blank*

Keep this in mind: If you have not created enough names for the last page, you might need to create some blank tickets at the end, after the merge is created, or add more names to the .csv file and redo the merge.

Creating the Final PDF for Print

If you're happy with the merge, you can save it and make final adjustments. Print the file or save it as a PDF for your printer as described in Chapter 2.

Alternately you could export the Data Merge file to PDF. Review Chapter 3 if you're not sure how to do this. On the Data Merge panel shortcut menu, select Export To PDF, as shown in Figure 5-18.

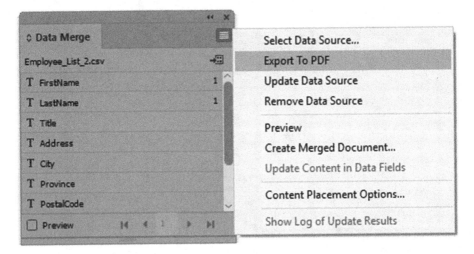

Figure 5-18. *On the Data Merge panel shortcut menu, select Export To PDF*

In the Export To PDF dialog box, click Export.

Save the file as Raffle_10_upMerge_End1b.pdf in the desired location and click Save, as shown in Figure 5-19.

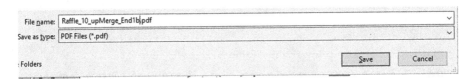

Figure 5-19. *Saving the multiple merge PDF file in a folder*

Through this method you might get the warning shown in Figure 5-20 about overset text. However, it is only seeing it with Preview mode set in the off state, so click OK.

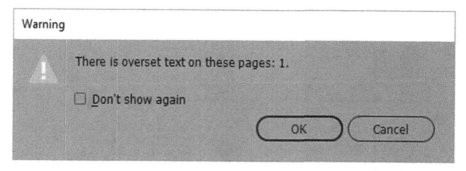

Figure 5-20. *An overset text warning*

Now a report will be generated as you left this setting selected on the Records tab.
In the Overset Text Report dialog box, shown in Figure 5-21, click Close and ignore this next message, as it is still referring to the Preview mode in an off state.

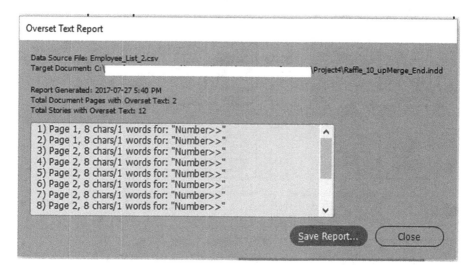

Figure 5-21. *An overset text report is generated*

With either method you will now be able to review your PDF in Adobe Acrobat Pro DC.

■ **Note**   As with single merges, you can add images or QR codes to multiple records. Check out the Mineral_Cards10up_MergeEnd.indd file I created using the mineral images shown in Figure 5-22.

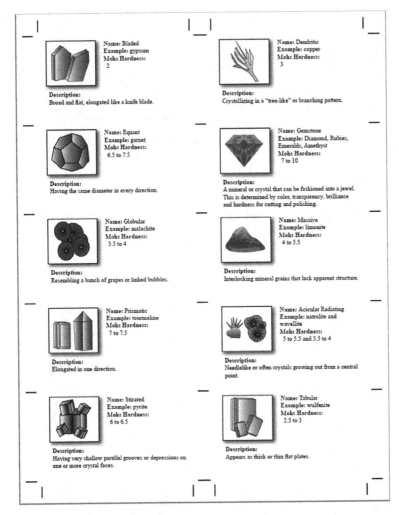

Figure 5-22. *An example of multiple records that could be used for info or business cards*

Final Thoughts and Using Sequential Numbering

You might have noticed that in my numbering on the raffle ticket I used random employee numbers rather than sequential numbers in Chapter 2.

You can create sequential numbering in MS Excel and later change it to a .csv file.

Select the first cell, A2, in the range that you want to fill. Right-click the cell and select Format Cells, as shown in Figure 5-23.

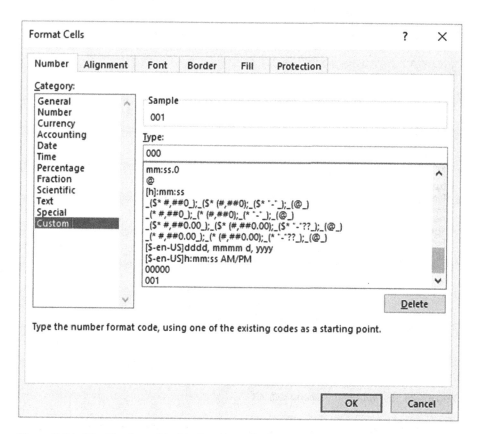

Figure 5-23. *Choose the cell that you want to format in Excel*

In the Format Cells dialog box, shown in Figure 5-24, set the Category to Custom and Type to 000. Click OK to exit the Format Cells dialog box.

Figure 5-24. *The Number tabl of the Format Cells dialog box*

The number 1 will now look like the display in Figure 5-25.

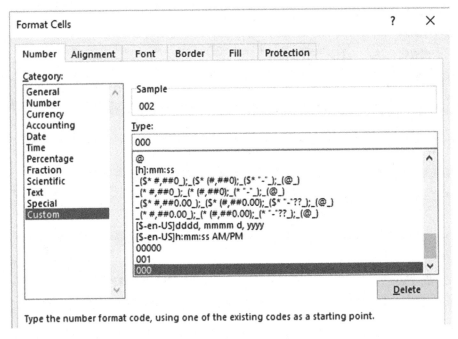

Figure 5-25. *The number now starts at 001*

In the next row, cell A3, add a 2 and give it the same format of Custom, as shown in Figure 5-26.

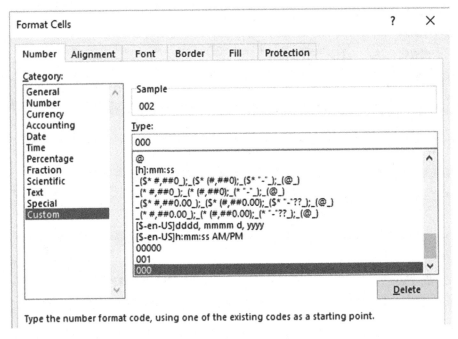

Figure 5-26. *Formating the second cell, A3*

Now press Shift and mouse click to select both cells. Use the green handle to drag downward until you have created enough numbers. If you need more, make sure to select all number cells before dragging on the green handle again to create more rows. Refer to Figure 5-27.

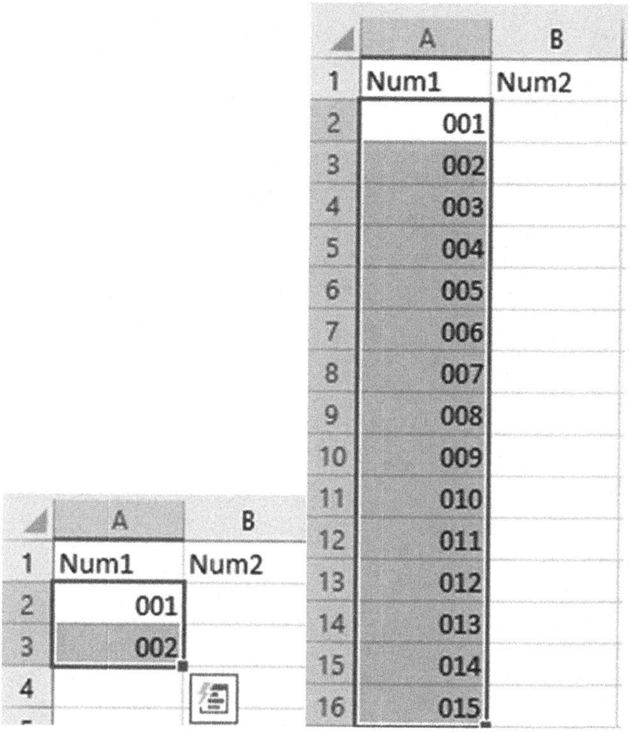

Figure 5-27. A column of sequential numbers

If you need the numbers twice for some reason, as displayed in Figure 5-28, you can select the numbers in the column and copy and paste them into the next column. However, in most cases you will only need one set that you can add twice via Data Merge in InDesign.

	A	B
1	Num1	Num2
2	001	001
3	002	002
4	003	003
5	004	004
6	005	005
7	006	006
8	007	007
9	008	008
10	009	009
11	010	010
12	011	011
13	012	012
14	013	013
15	014	014
16	015	015

Figure 5-28. *Two columns of sequential numbers*

Save the file as a .csv file, as in Chapter 3, and close the file. You can check if the numbering sequence has been retained in NotePad++ (see Figure 5-29). However, do not open the .csv file again in Excel or the formatting will be lost and you will need to create a new .csv file.

```
Num1,Num2
001,001
002,002
003,003
```

Figure 5-29. *View the numbering in NotePad++*

Now if you have a ticket that requires sequential numbering along with names, you know how to create this type of file for your Data Merge.

Can I Make Calculations with Expression Fields Like Word?

Microsoft Word with Excel can make extra math calculations with the data from a mail merge using expression fields. However, you cannot accomplish this in InDesign without advanced knowledge in GREPS and scripting. If you have custom calculations, you could choose the Word method or make the adjustments to your calculations using formulas in your Excel file first and save the data as a .csv for InDesign CC.

Additional Resources

If you want to create Charts and Graphs in InDesign using your Data Merge here, are some links you can check out about a product called Chartwell:

- https://indesignsecrets.com/grep-style-bar-graphs-for-data-merge.php

- http://indesignsecrets.com/creating-charts-graphs-automagically-data-merge-chartwell.php

Summary

In this chapter, you discovered how to place multiple records on one page for a Data Merge. As with single data merges, it is possible to use Paragraph styles to style the resultant Data Merge text. You also saw that you can add numbering, images, and QR codes to multiple merges.

In the next chapter, you will be looking at how to use Character styles and Paragraph style GREPS to alter your text further when you encounter differences in information, such as employee titles and price changes.

■ ■ ■

Working with Character and Paragraph GREP Styles with the Data Merge Panel

Project: Creating Name Cards for Tables and Creating an Alert Color When information Changes in a Customized Letter with Prices

---

■ **Note**   If you want to work along in this lesson or review the result, download your Chapter 6 files from http://www.apress.com/9781484231586. Work with the file with the label "Start." The file with the label "End" and the PDFs are the final result.

In Chapter 2, you briefly looked at how an expression such as ^# could affect the way numbers format in a ticket numbering list. You also discovered at the end of Chapter 5 that unlike Microsoft Word, you could not make calculations with expression fields. You need to use Microsoft Excel to perform complex math formulas and then convert the data to a .csv file, which can be viewed in InDesign via Data Merge. However, what if after all your work, like in Figure 6-1, you still want certain words like personal titles or price ranges to display differently?

© Jennifer Harder 2017
J. Harder, *Data Merge and Styles for Adobe InDesign CC 2018*,
https://doi.org/10.1007/978-1-4842-3159-3_6

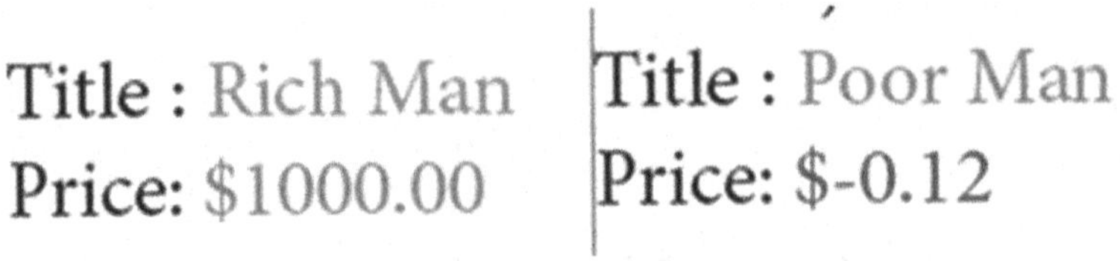

Title : Rich Man   Title : Poor Man
Price: $1000.00   Price: $-0.12

Figure 6-1. Titles and prices changing color

This is the power of GREP styles!

What Are GREPs?

In InDesign, this acronym stands for global/regular expressions/print. There are many web sites and books written on the topic. People who design web sites will know of them as Regular Expressions (RegExp). I even talk about Regular Expressions for formatting and validation in my book *Enhancing Adobe Acrobat DC Forms with JavaScript*. GREPs are a type of a program language that scans a specified file or files line by line, returning lines that contain a pattern. From an InDesign point of view, here are some links you can look at to become familiar with GREPs:

- https://helpx.adobe.com/indesign/using/find-change.html
- https://helpx.adobe.com/indesign/using/drop-caps-nested-styles.html
- http://indesignsecrets.com/topic/using-grep-to-select-a-number-range
- http://indesignsecrets.com/favorite-grep-expressions-you-can-use.php
- http://indesignsecrets.com/6-cool-things-you-can-do-with-grep-styles.php
- http://indesignsecrets.com/resources/grep

After viewing these links, you might have concluded that GREPs are powerful for formatting. However, if you aren't familiar with programming language, it can be complicated and confusing. You are right. I think becoming an expert at all things GREPs would take years to master. Thankfully, everything starts with small steps, so let's try a few things. For this lesson, let's first apply it to some table place cards for an event.

Open Adobe InDesign CC

To begin, open the InDesign CC 2018. If you have not already set up your workspace, make sure to go back to Chapter 1 and review the information on creating a workspace for the Data Merge. Otherwise, select the Data Merge Workspace or Reset Data Merge Workspace from the InDesign drop-down menu, as shown in Figure 6-2.

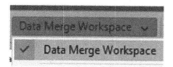

Figure 6-2. *The InDesign workspace that you will be using for this chapter*

If you were beginning the files from scratch, you would choose File ➤ New Document and begin laying out the text and graphics that you might have created in Photoshop or Illustrator. However, for this chapter, choose File ➤ Open to open the document (Table_Cards_Start.indd) in the Chapter 6 folder, which is the file that contains the layout I have already created (see Figures 6-3 and 6-4).

Figure 6-3. *Table card example*

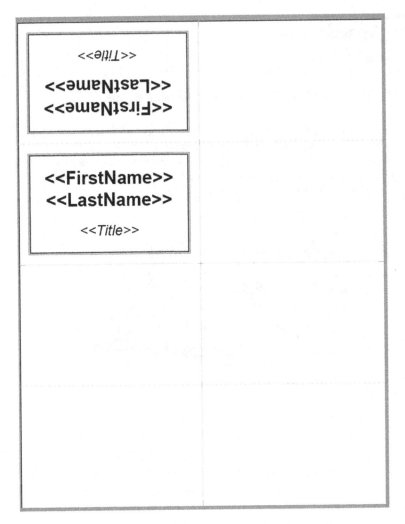

Figure 6-4. Table cards that can be four-up on a sheet for an event

In this case I have created a four-up layout of some table cards. When the cards are folded, the guests name will be on the front and the back of the folded card.

File Setup Review

The Layers panel (Window ➤ Layers) reveals that there are two layers. The CropMarks layer contains the crop marks and folding lines. The lines are found on the Pages panel (Window ➤ Pages) in the A-Master. Refer to Figure 6-5.

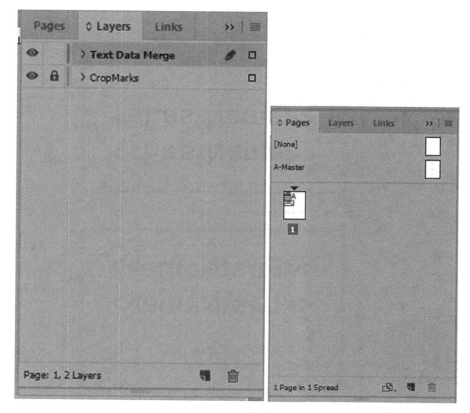

Figure 6-5. *The Layers and Pages panels for this document with the crop marks on the Master page and in the CropMarks layer*

I added the crop marks to the Master Page as in Chapter 5, because you are going to create a multimerged record and you do not want the marks to move with the other items. I then locked the CropMarks layer (see Figure 6-5).

The Text Data Merge layer contains the Data Merge text and background.

Using the Selection tool (V), draw a marquee around all the items and select Object ➤ Group or Ctrl+G or Command+G and group them as one object so that it will move as one item in the Data Merge (see Figure 6-6). If you don't do this, the front and back of the table card might display two different names.

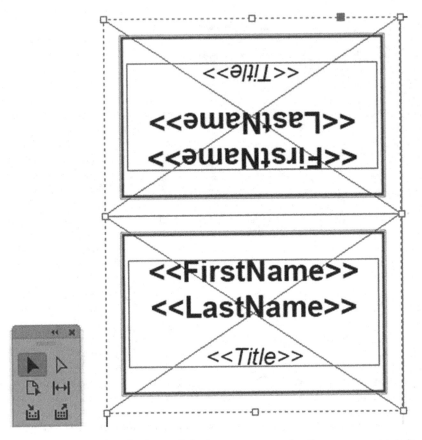

Figure 6-6. Using the Selection tool, the items are grouped so they move as one unit

The Data Merge Panel

As you can see, a Data Merge is already set up in Figure 6-7. You have selected my data source (Employee_List_project5.csv) from the Data Merge drop-down menu.

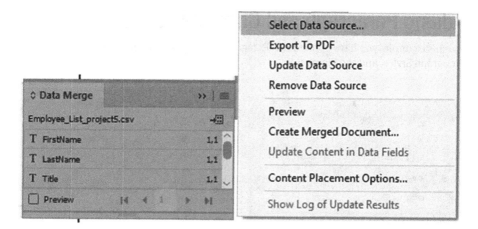

Figure 6-7. *The Data Merge panel is set up with the correct fields*

When you click through the Data Merge panel preview, you can view the different names that will appear on the table cards, as shown in Figure 6-8.

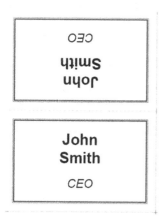

Figure 6-8. *How the table cards appear in Data Merge Preview mode*

Adding Paragraph and Character Styles

For this example, you have applied two Paragraph styles. Go to Window ➤ Styles ➤ Paragraph Styles, and see Figure 6-9.

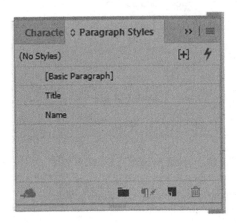

Figure 6-9. Two Paragraph styles are found in the document: Title and Name for each guest

Name is the field for the first and last name of the guest and Title is for the guest's job title. In your own personal project, you could use a company name or an organization instead.

In this case you want to apply distinct colors to the job titles. When you cycle through you only get one color that was applied using the Character Color setting in the Paragraph Style Options dialog box shown in Figure 6-10. How can you alter that?

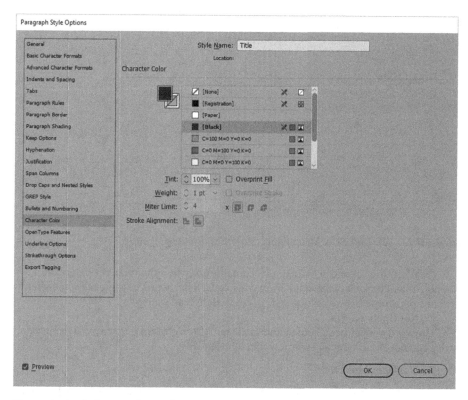

Figure 6-10. *Only one color and stroke can be applied on the Paragraph Style Options dialog box Character Color tab*

■ **Tip** If you need to differentiate between several vendors, this is a great idea for name badges or place cards.

Close the Paragraph Style Options dialog box if you have opened it.

The Character Styles Panel and Dialog Box

Click in the pasteboard area so that no text is selected and go to Window ➤ Styles ➤ Character Styles to open the Character Styles panel in Figure 6-11.

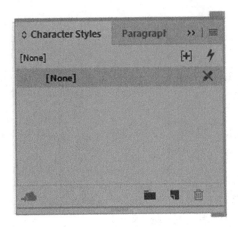

Figure 6-11. *The Character Styles panel currently with no syles added*

Currently the Character Styles panel contains no styles other than the default of [None]. Character styles are useful when you need a letter, word, or sentence somewhere within a paragraph to be a unique style or color. Here is an example:

Do **Not** Open this File!

The word not has been bolded and made red. If you created this style as a Paragraph styles and not as a Character style, it would look like this:

Do Not Open this File!

Notice that the whole paragraph becomes bolded and red, which might not be what you want.

With no text selected, click Create New Style at the bottom of the Character Styles panel, shown in Figure 6-12. Alternatively, you can use the drop-down menu in the upper right corner of the Character Styles panel to create a new Character style.

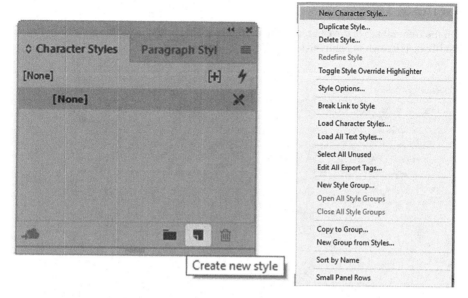

Figure 6-12. *On the Character Styles panel, click Create New Style*

Creating Character Styles

With the new style created, as shown in Figure 6-13, double-click it to open the Character Style Options dialog box.

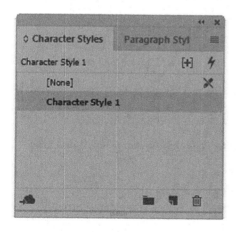

Figure 6-13. *The Character Styles panel with the new style created*

General Tab

On the General tab of the Character Style Options dialog box, change the Style Name to Red Text, as shown in Figure 6-14.

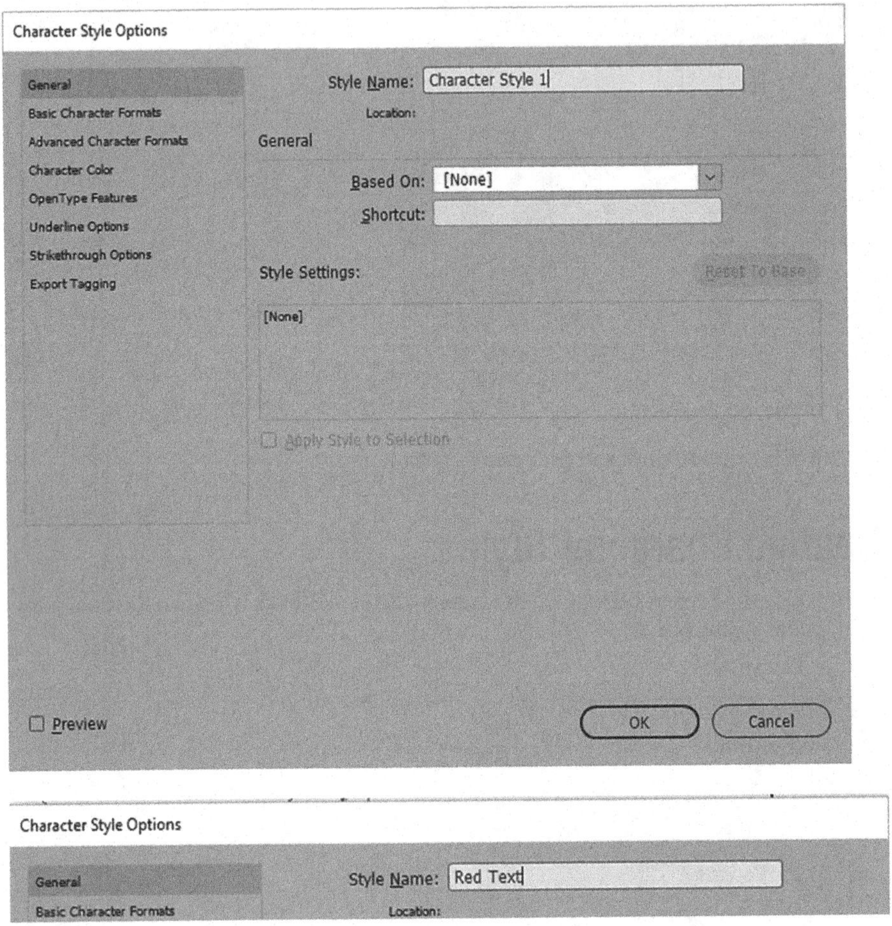

Figure 6-14. On the General tab of the Character Style Options dialog box, type a new style name

Leave all the other settings at their defaults.

In the General section, Based On should be set to [None] as you don't currently have any other styles to base the current Character style on. If you did you could select a style from the drop-down menu. You can use the Shortcut field if you want to create a keyboard shortcut to apply the style.

Style Settings provides an overview of all the style options applied; currently, there are none. However, this will change by the time you are finished with this dialog box.

The Apply Style to Selection check box can be selected or cleared, as can the Preview check box.

Character Color Tab

Click the Character Color tab shown in Figure 6-15. Inside the Character Color section, change the color to a red. This is a very similar layout to the Paragraph Style options.

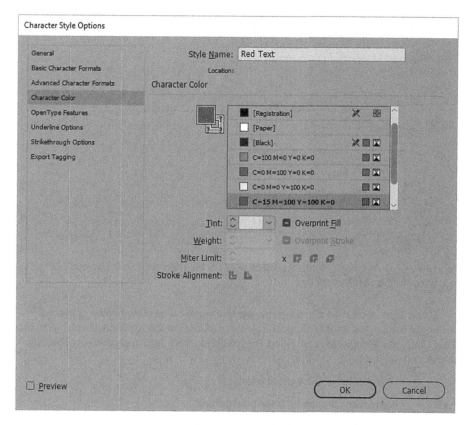

Figure 6-15. *Choosing a new color on the Character Color tab of the Character Style Options dialog box*

You can adjust the fill and stroke color of your characters as well as the tint, if the fill will overprint.

For the stroke, you can also adjust the Weight setting, if the stroke will overprint, Miter Limit, and Stroke Alignment.

At this time, on this tab, you will only change the color.

207

Basic Character Formats Tab

Click the Basic Character Formats tab to view this area, shown in Figure 6-16. Note this area is very like the Paragraph styles options in the Basic Character Formats section.

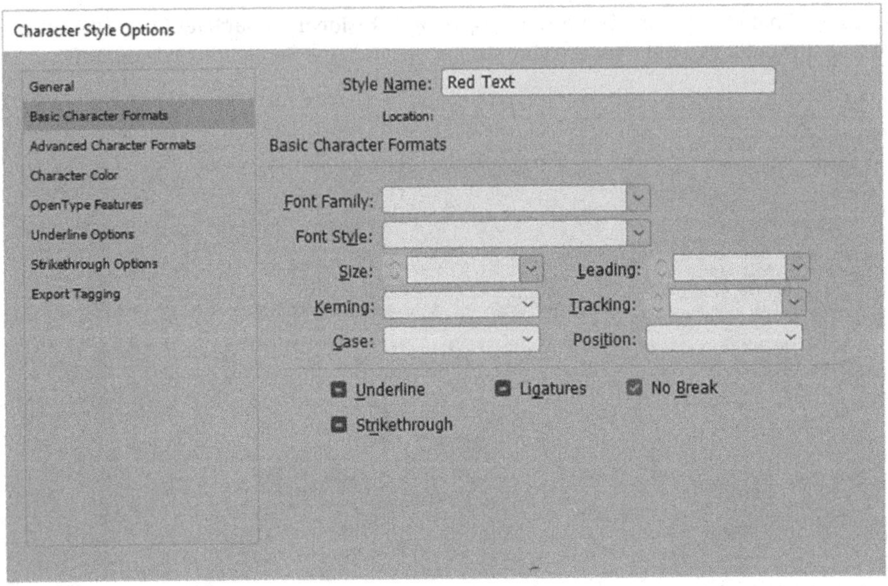

Figure 6-16. *On the Basic Character Formats tab of the Character Style Options dialog box, select the No Break check box*

If you were concerned that a specific word or phrase would hyphenate or overset during the merge, you could change the font size and select the No Break check box in the Basic Character Formats section. Select the No Break check box, and otherwise leave this area at its default settings.

- Font Family: Choose a font family.

- Font Style: This can be set to bold or italic.

- Size: This setting determines the font size.

- Leading, Kerning, and Tracking: These settings adjust the font spacing.

- Case: This can be set to Small Caps or All Caps.

- Position: This can be set to Subscript or Superscript.

- You can use the remaining check boxes to choose if the font will be underlined, will have ligatures, will have no break, or will have a strikethrough.

Other Options in the Character Styles Dialog Box

You might find the Advanced Character Formats tab useful for Data Merge.

Advanced Character Formats Tab

You can adjust the Vertical Scale, Horizontal Scale, Baseline Shift, and Skew settings for the text if you need to create a faux italic font. This tab, shown in Figure 6-17, is like the one found in the Paragraph styles.

Character Style Options

General
Basic Character Formats
Advanced Character Formats
Character Color
OpenType Features
Underline Options
Strikethrough Options
Export Tagging

Style Name: Red Text
Location:

Advanced Character Formats

Horizontal Scale:
Vertical Scale:
Baseline Shift:
Skew:

Language:

Figure 6-17. Advanced Character Formats tab of the Character Style Options dialog box

You will leave the other tabs at their default settings, as they do not apply to this project. Click OK and close the Character Style Options dialog box for now.

You will now have the new style, Red Text, added to the list, as shown in Figure 6-18.

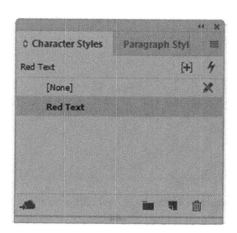

Figure 6-18. Inside the Character Styles panel, a new style has been added

You will now create three more Character styles: Blue Text, Green Text, and Yellow Text.

With the Red Text Character style still selected, from the drop-down menu select Duplicate Style, as shown in Figure 6-19.

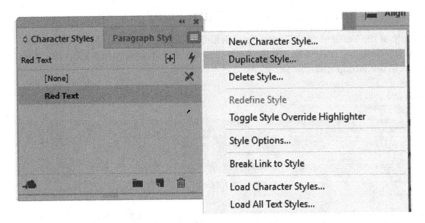

Figure 6-19. *Duplcating a Paragraph style*

On the General tab of the Duplicate Style dialog box (see Figure 6-20), change the Style Name setting to Blue Text. From the Based On list box, select Red Text to keep any other formatting line breaks.

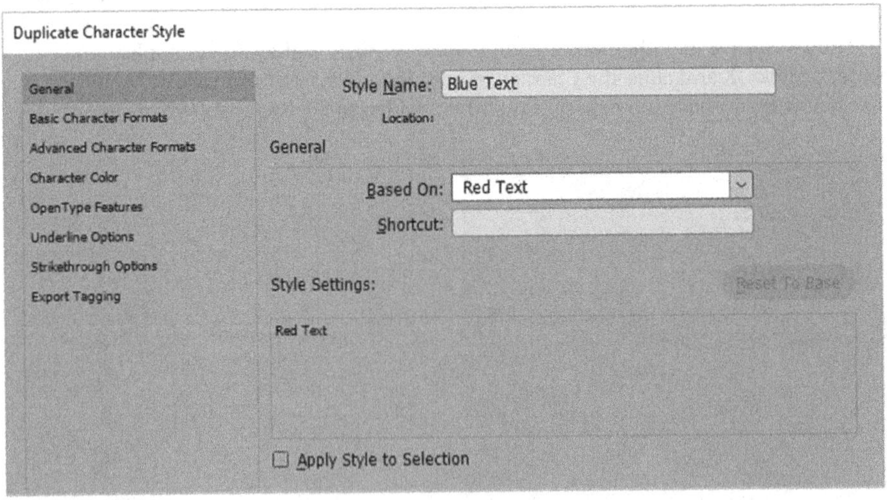

Figure 6-20. *Change the name and what it is based on for the duplicated Character style on the General tab*

Next, click the Character Color tab, shown in Figure 6-21. There, change the Character Color setting to a blue.

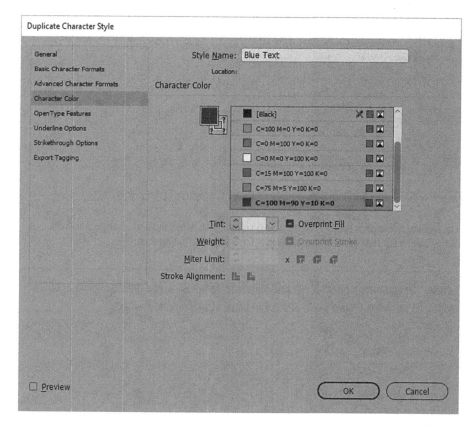

Figure 6-21. *Change the character color of the duplicated Character style on the Character Color tab*

Click OK when done to close the Duplicate Character Style dialog box. You should now have two Character styles, shown in Figure 6-22.

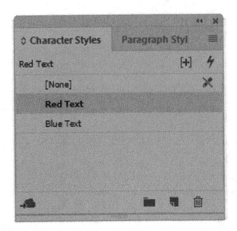

Figure 6-22. *Two styles are now available in the Character Styles panel*

Repeat the earlier steps for green and yellow text. Make sure to change the style name, base it on Red Text, and change the Character Color setting.

■ **Note** In your own project if you find yellow to be too light, feel free to choose another color or, as shown in Figure 6-23, add a thin black stroke around the text.

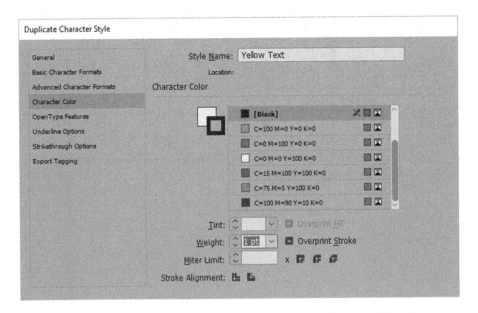

Figure 6-23. *Add a black stroke around the yellow text on the Character Color tab*

You should now have the four Character styles shown in Figure 6-24.

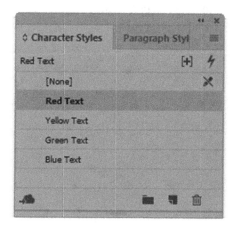

Figure 6-24. *Four styles are now available in the Character Styles panel*

Applying Character Styles to a Specific Pattern or Word Using Paragraph Style GREPs

Most people, when they use Character styles, highlight a section of text within a paragraph and then apply a Character style. Although this method is good for simple documents, it does not allow you to change the color of the text during the Data Merge, if the wording changes. Data Merges are all about conformity and customization, so you do not apply Character styles in the way I just described. Instead, you select the base style of [None] for all the text in this file, as shown in Figure 6-25.

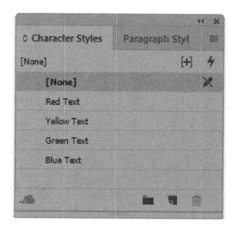

Figure 6-25. *While no text is selected, in the Character Styles panel, select [None]*

Paragraph Styles Panel

Now you will return the Paragraph Styles panel, shown in Figure 6-26. Make sure no text is selected.

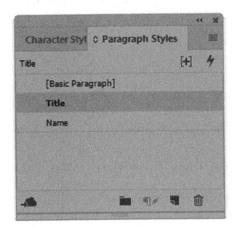

Figure 6-26. *Return to the Paragraph Styles panel*

Double-click the Title style and click the GREP Style tab in the Paragraph Style Options dialog box.

GREP Style Tab

On the GREP Styles tab, shown in Figure 6-27, you will apply your new Character styles.

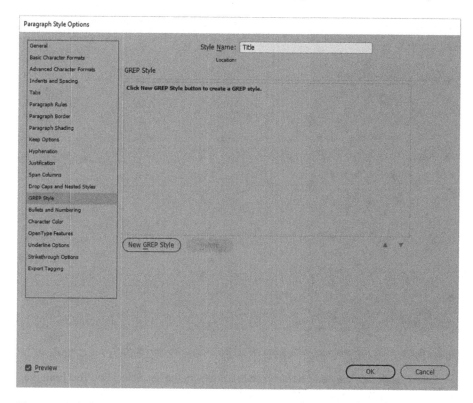

Figure 6-27. *The GREP Style tab of the Paragraph Style Options dialog box*

Using this method, you can ensure that a certain word won't break, is appears in bold type, or appears in colored type. Here in the Titles Paragraph style that you applied to your Titles line, you can make various titles of people appear in distinct colors.

Click New GREP Style, shown in Figure 6-28. This opens the dialog box shown in Figure 6-29.

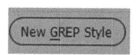

Figure 6-28. *The New GREP Style button*

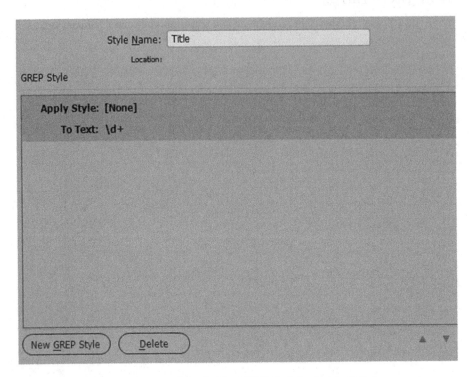

Figure 6-29. This line appears when the New GREP Style button is clicked

Select an already created Character style color from the list. Select Red Text from the Apply Style drop-down list, as shown in Figure 6-30.

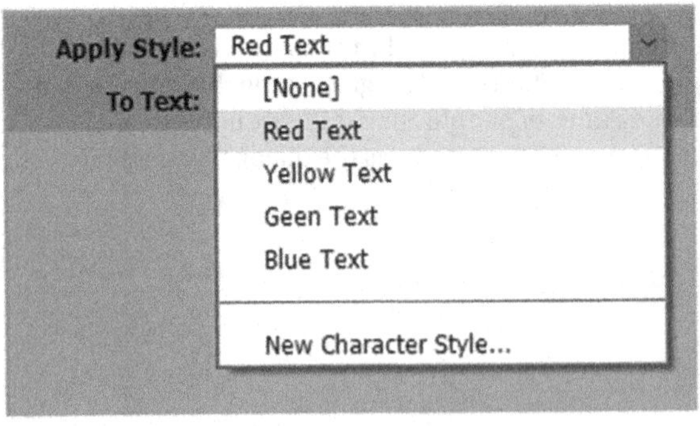

Figure 6-30. Apply a Character style from the Apply Style drop-down list

In the To Text text box, enter the name of the title that comes from the `.csv` file you want to affect. For this example, use the title CEO, as shown in Figure 6-31.

Figure 6-31. *Apply the style to the word you want to affect*

■ **Note** There are many other GREP combinations to choose from under the @ symbol (see Figure 6-32). Not all will work with Data Merge, but it's good to experiment. See the links on the first page of this tutorial for details on each GREP. Also, check out Table 6-1 at the end of this chapter.

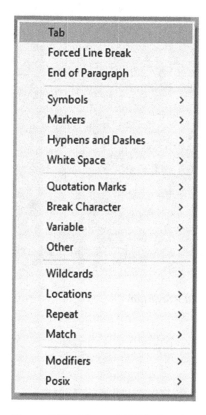

Figure 6-32. *Menu of GREPs found under the @ symbol icon*

Add three more new GREP styles:

- Apply Style: Blue Text
  To Text: Manager

- Apply Style: Green Text
  To Text: Sales Representative

- Apply Style: Yellow Text
  To Text: Geologist

The result is shown in Figure 6-33.

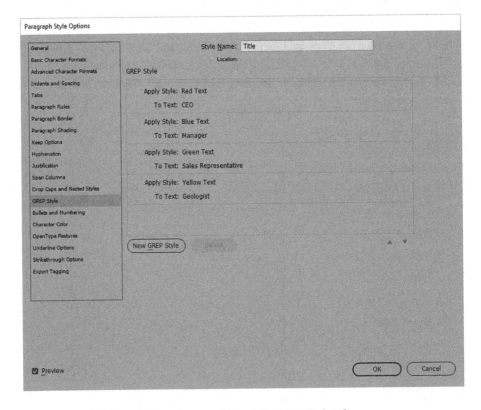

Figure 6-33. All the styles have been applied on the GREP Style tab

If you don't like a GREP that was created, you can select it and click Delete. The up and down arrows on the right side allow you to reorder your styles. If you rename a Character style in the Character Styles panel, it will automatically rename itself here so you do not need to update.

You can create a new style from the Apply Style drop-down list. Select New Character Style, as shown in Figure 6-34, to open the Character Style Options dialog box.

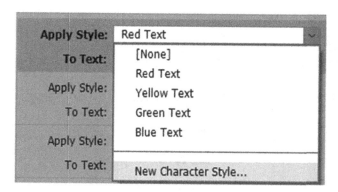

Figure 6-34. *Create a new Character style directly from the GREPs Style tab*

This new style can later be accessed in the Character Styles panel. When you are done, click OK to close the Paragraph Styles menu.

Now take a moment to click Preview in the Data Merge panel. Notice when you sort through the Data Merge the titles of each person display in different colors, as shown in Figure 6-35.

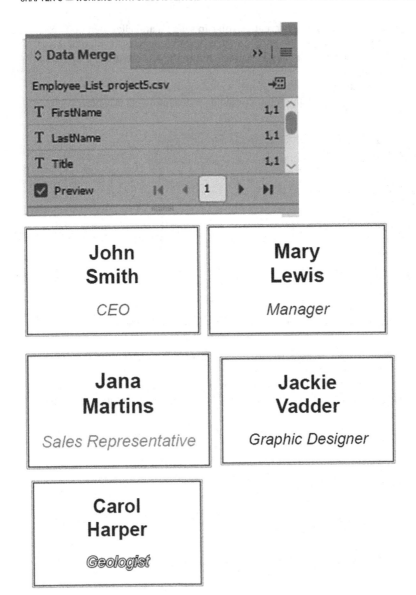

Figure 6-35. Select the Preview check box to see all the new colors the Character styles created

The Graphic Designer title did not change color because you did not give that name a style. Likewise, if a title had been misspelled in the .csv it would have remained at the default color. This is an effective way of prechecking for errors in your Data Merge.

You'll adjust one more Paragraph Styles panel tab in this file before you finish the Data Merge.

Drop Caps and Nested Styles Tab

Suppose that you liked the black outline that appeared around the yellow text and you wanted this outline for all the titles. You could go into each Character style and make this change or you could use the Drop Caps and Nested Styles tab of the Paragraph Style Options dialog box.

With no text selected, double-click the Title style in the Paragraph Styles panel and click the Drop Caps and Nested Styles tab shown in Figure 6-36.

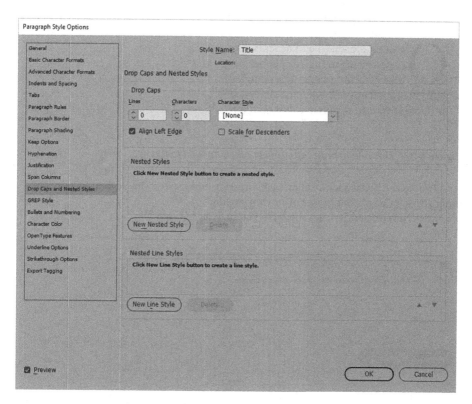

Figure 6-36. *Double-click on the Paragraph style Title and click the Drop Caps and Nested Styles tab*

The Drop Caps and Nested Styles tab allows you to add a drop cap style to the beginning of a paragraph with a specific Character style. You can also select the Align the Left Edge and Scale for Descenders check boxes shown in Figure 6-37.

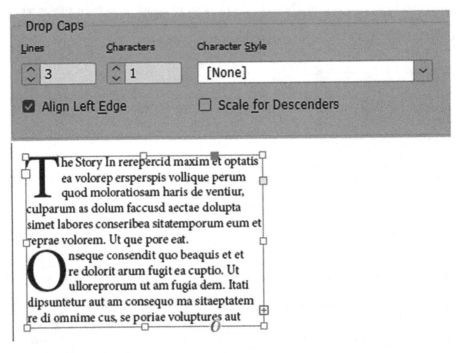

Figure 6-37. *This is how drop caps appear when applied to text*

The Nested Styles section allows you override other styles with additional parts of other styles for words or phrases of varying lengths.

Click New Nested Style, as shown in Figure 6-38.

Figure 6-38. *Nested Styles section of the Drop Caps and Nested Styles tab*

Select the Yellow Text Character style and make sure that it goes through two words by entering the number in the field, as shown in Figure 6-39. Use this setting because all the titles have at least two words and you want the outline to go around all the words in the title.

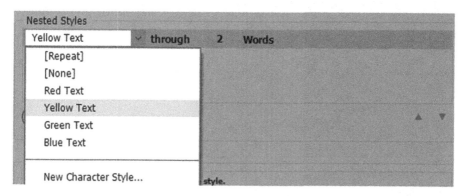

Figure 6-39. *Nested Styles section on the Drop Caps and Nested Styles tab. Apply the Character style that contains a stroke*

■ **Note** In the Through drop-down list, you can choose either Through or Up to, as shown in Figure 6-40.

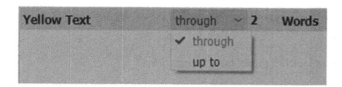

Figure 6-40. *Two options on the Through drop-down menu on the Drop Caps and Nested Styles tab*

On the Words drop-down menu, there are a variety of other choices that you could use for your own project, such as Letters or Digits. Figure 6-41 shows this menu.

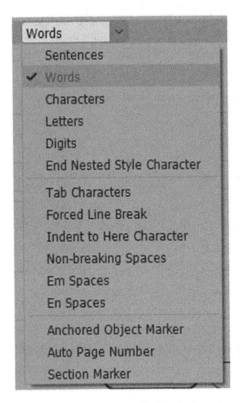

Figure 6-41. *Options on the Words drop-down menu on the Drop Caps and Nested Styles tab*

Your settings should now look like those shown in Figure 6-42.

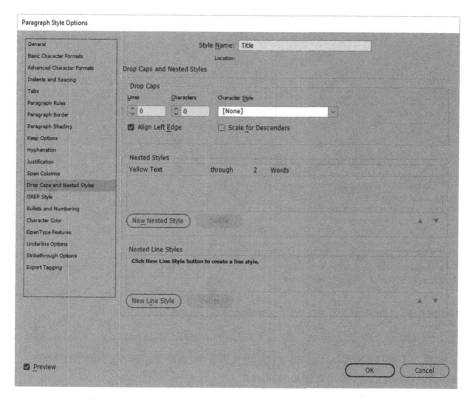

Figure 6-42. *Final settings for the Paragraph style Title on the Drop Caps and Nested Styles tab*

The other section, Nested Line Style, affects how many lines the style flows on to, as shown in Figure 6-43.

Nested Line Styles

| Character Style 1 | for | 2 | lines |

New Line Style   Delete   ▲ ▼

The Story In rerepercid maxim et optatis ea volorep ersperspis vollique perum quod moloratiosam haris de ventiur, culparum as dolum faccusd aectae dolupta simet labores conseribea sitatemporum eum et reprae volorem. Ut que pore eat.

Onseque consendit quo beaquis et et re dolorit arum fugit ea cuptio. Ut ullore-prorum ut am fugia dem. Itati dipsun-tetur aut am consequo ma sitaeptatem re di omnime cus, se poriae voluptures aut quunti-

Figure 6-43. *How text appears when a nested line style is added*

___

■ **Note** if you've added a nested or line style that you want to remove, select the style and click Delete under each area to remove it.

___

Click OK to close the Paragraph Style Options dialog box. When you preview the Data Merge with the Preview check box selected, you should now see the outline applied to all titles. Notice in Figure 6-44 that the Graphic Designer title is now yellow because it had no GREP style applied and this nested style has overridden it.

Jana Martins

Sales Representative

Jackie Vadder

Graphic Designer

Figure 6-44. *How text appears now that the nested style has been applied*

Now you will prepare for the multimerge.

Return to the Data Merge Panel

On the Data Merge panel, from the drop-down menu, select Create Merged Document, as shown in Figure 6-45. Refer to Chapter 5 if you need to review this process.

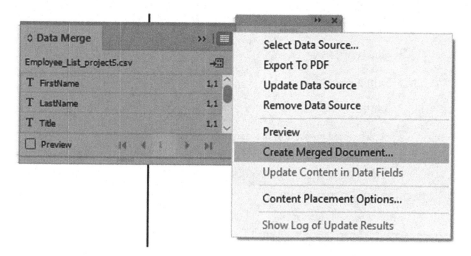

Figure 6-45. *In the Data Merge panel select Create Merged Document*

On the Records tab, set the Records per Document Page drop-down list to Multiple Records, as shown in Figure 6-46.

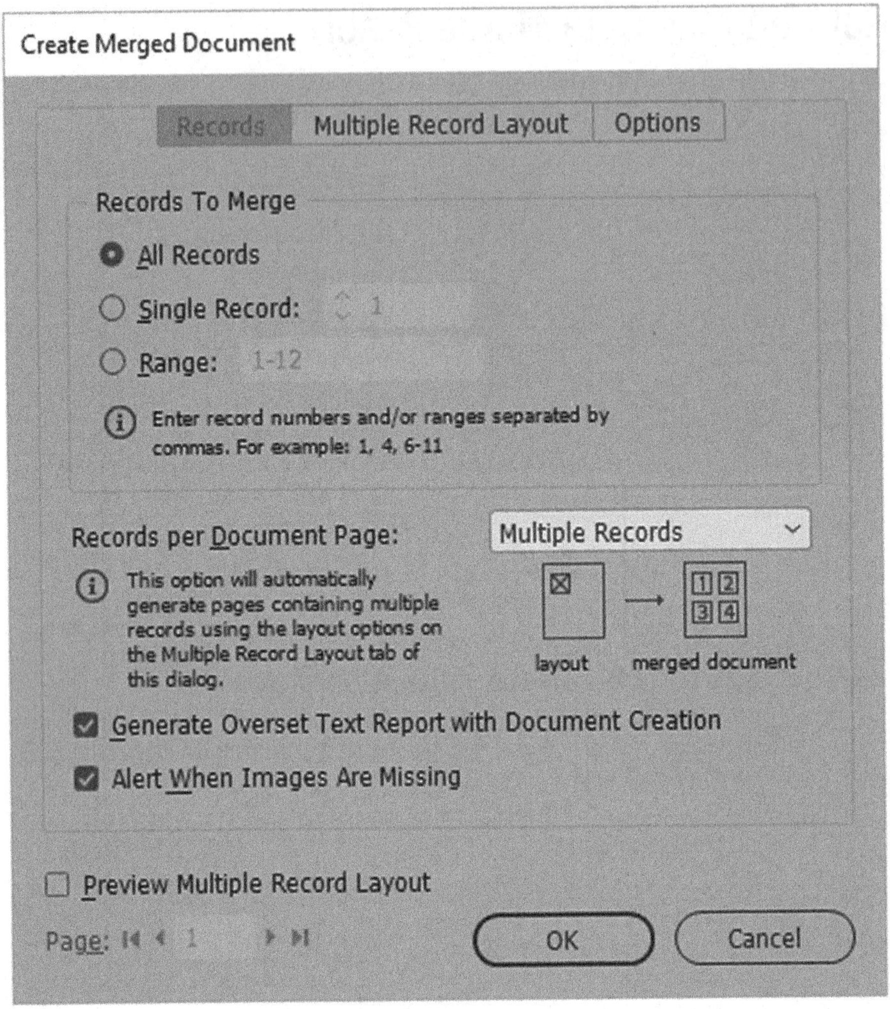

Create Merged Document

| Records | Multiple Record Layout | Options |

Records To Merge

● All Records

○ Single Record: ⇕ 1

○ Range: 1-12

ⓘ Enter record numbers and/or ranges separated by
commas. For example: 1, 4, 6-11

Records per Document Page: Multiple Records ⌄

ⓘ This option will automatically
generate pages containing multiple
records using the layout options on
the Multiple Record Layout tab of
this dialog.

⊠ → [1][2]
      [3][4]

layout   merged document

☑ Generate Overset Text Report with Document Creation

☑ Alert When Images Are Missing

☐ Preview Multiple Record Layout

Page: |◀ ◀ 1 ▶ ▶| (OK)   (Cancel)

Figure 6-46. On the Records tab of the Create Merged Document dialog box, select Multiple Records from the Records per Document Page drop-down list

On the Multiple Record Layout tab, set the settings shown in Figure 6-47. Select the Preview Multiple Record Layout check box to see if the table cards are setting up in a four-up pattern.

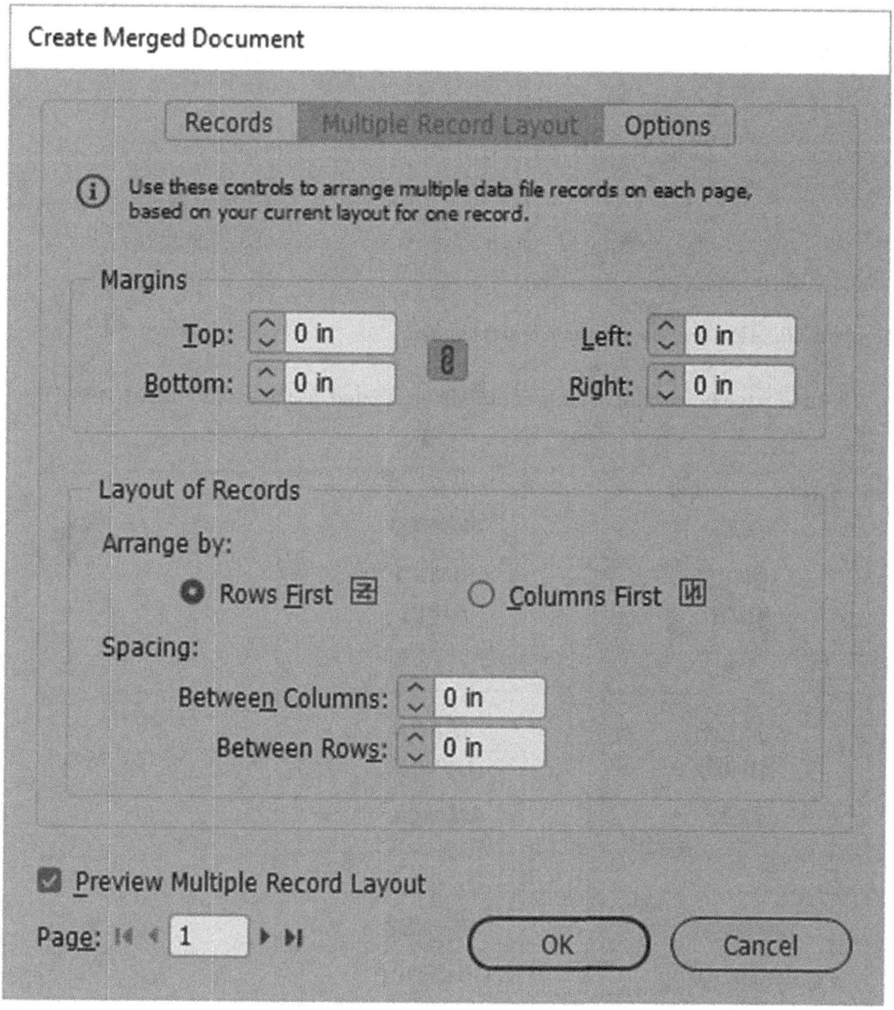

Figure 6-47. *On the Multiple Record Layout tab of the Create Merged Document dialog box, select the Preview Multiple Records Layout check box to see if the settings have altered correctly for the layout*

You do not need to adjust anything on the Options tab. However, if your own project had images connected to the .csv file, you might have to adjust that tab.

When you are done, click OK to let the Data Merge create a new file. You will receive the alert displayed in Figure 6-48 about no overset text. Click OK to dimiss the alert.

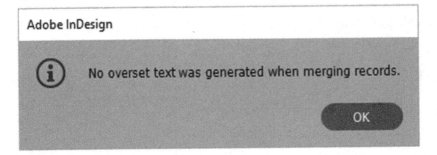

Figure 6-48. *Alert that no overset text was created*

A three-page document of table cards will be created, as shown in Figure 6-49.

Figure 6-49. *Page one of the table cards generated from the Data Merge*

Export to PDF

You can now create a PDF for print using the method covered in Chapter 2 or the method detailed in Chapter 3. In the Data Merge panel, select Export To PDF, as shown in Figure 6-50.

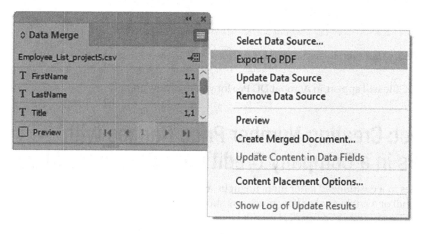

Figure 6-50. *Use the Data Merge panel drop-down menu to export a file to a PDF*

With either method, you will be asked to save the file in your folder and click Save. Save the file as Table_Cards_End-1a.pdf as shown in Figure 6-51.

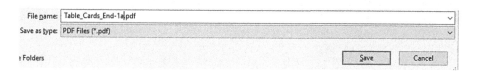

Figure 6-51. *Save the file as a PDF in your folder*

Click OK to dismiss the no overset text warning shown in Figure 6-52.

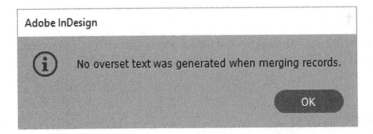

Figure 6-52. Alert that no overset text was created

A PDF file will appear in Acrobat DC Pro for you to review and print.

Project: Creating Number Price Ranges with GREPs in a Company Credit Card Payment Notice

Sometimes in a customized letter there might be an area telling you how much you still owe on a bill or a credit card or how much you should make for a minimum payment before the interest rate goes up next month.

In this example, I show you how to style the font in distinct colors using number ranges and GREPs styles.

Open the File in InDesign

Open the file PriceMerge_Start.indd in the Chapter 6 folder. The document will look like Figure 6-53.

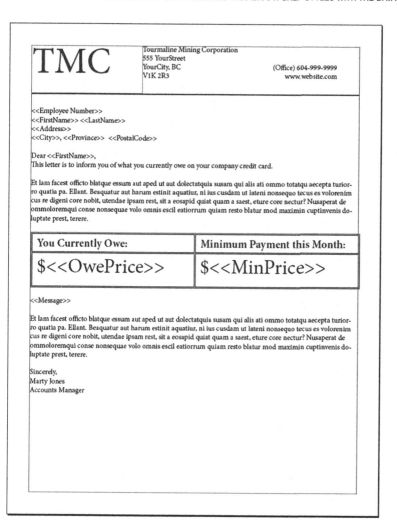

Figure 6-53. *Credit card letter example*

In this example, you are returning to the single Data Merge as you used in Chapter 3.

Review the Applied Styles

However, this letter has two new areas, a table that I styled using Table styles and Cell styles. To access these, settings, go to Window ➤ Styles ➤ Table Styles and Window ➤ Styles ➤ Cell Styles, respectively. You can double-click on each style, shown in Figure 6-54, to see the options I used. Click OK to close them.

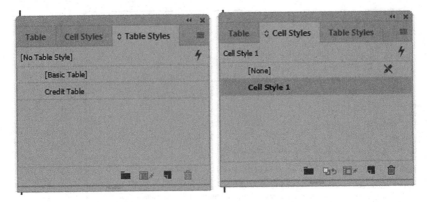

Figure 6-54. *Styles created in the Table Styles and Cell Styles panels*

Table styles affect the outer styling of the table, whereas Cell styles affect the inner styling of the table.

The table by itself does not play any part in the Data Merge, other than I dragged the Data Merge fields shown in Figure 6-55 into the table.

You Currently Owe:	Minimum Payment this Month:
$<<OwePrice>>	$<<MinPrice>>

Figure 6-55. *Data Merge fields in the table*

Previewing the Styles with the Data Merge Panel

I applied a style to each field called Owe Text and Min Payment Text (see Figure 6-56). You will style the Owe Text with color and number ranges.

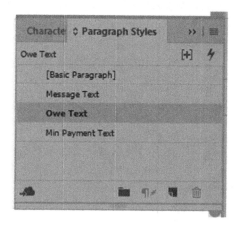

Figure 6-56. *Altering the Owe Text style in the Paragraph Styles panel*

■ **Note**   The Message Text style is for the message that will appear under the table.

Select the Preview check box on the Data Merge panel to view the current file. Notice that all the text is black and does not change color. When you are finished looking though the results with the arrow icons, clear the Preview check box and click on the pasteboard so that no text is currently selected. Refer to Figure 6-57.

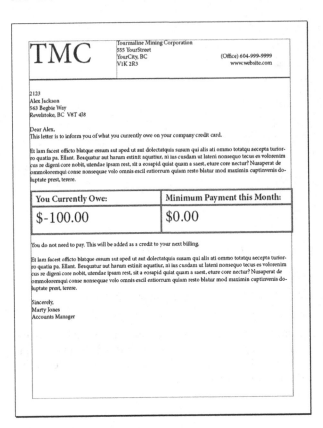

Figure 6-57.   Previewing the merge with the Data Merge panel. All text is black

Setting the Number Ranges

Let's begin by importing the Character styles from the last table card project.

Open your Character Styles panel and from the drop-down menu, select Load Character Styles, as shown in Figure 6-58.

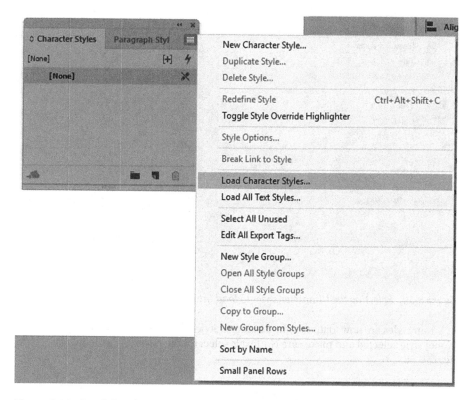

Figure 6-58. *Load the Character styles into the Character Styles panel*

Find the Table_Cards_End.indd file. Make sure the Red Text, Yellow Text, Green Text, and Blue Text Character styles are selected and all Paragraph styles are cleared, as displayed in Figure 6-59. Click OK to load the styles.

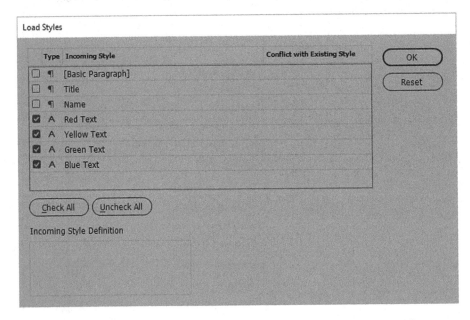

Figure 6-59. *Selecting the Character styles to load into the Character Styles panel*

Your styles are now loaded in the Character Styles panel. Make sure to keep the [None] style selected and make sure No Text is select for the next step, as shown in Figure 6-60.

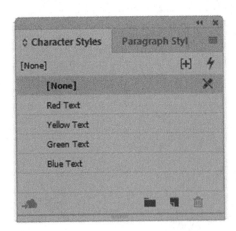

Figure 6-60. *The Character styles are now loaded into the panel*

Now you want to alter the <<OwePrice>> field. You will use the same colors in a different combination. However, this time you will use actual GREPs to alter the range. You have ensured that when your price is negative it is shown in blue (they owe nothing) and when it is positive it displays in red (they owe someone money).

In the Paragraph Styles panel, select the Owe Text style, as shown in Figure 6-61.

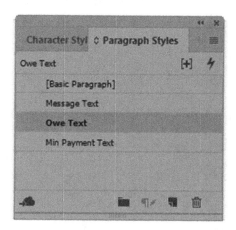

Figure 6-61. *Double-click to open the Paragraph Style Options dialog box for the Owe Text style*

Click the GREP Style tab and enter the two new GREP styles shown in Figure 6-62.

- For Red Text, To Text: \$\d+\.\d\d

- For Blue Text, To Text: \$\-\d+\.\d\d

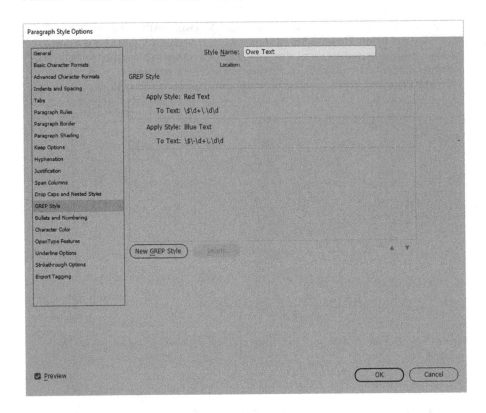

Figure 6-62. *On the GREP Style tab of the Paragraph Style Options dialog box, add two new GREP styles*

Click OK to exit the Paragraph Style Options dialog box.
Preview the results using the Data Merge panel. They should look like Figure 6-63.

You Currently Owe:	Minimum Payment this Month:
$90.06	$10.00

You Currently Owe:	Minimum Payment this Month:
$-100.00	$0.00

Figure 6-63. *Notice how the numbers change color if they are positive or negative*

Here's a brief explanation of the code. Although it would take several hours to explain all GREPs, the ones I used in the example mean this.

Example: $1000.00

\means an escape to the next symbol, in this case $. You need to do this for the code to work because the $ by itself in some cases has an alternate meaning. Refer Table 6-1 at the end of the chapter.

\d means digit or a number. For example, to type 5\d would be a number between 50 and 59.

\d+ means a length of digits or number, but you don't know how many; it could be a $1.00, $10.00, $1000.00, and so on. Whatever is coming from the Data Merge, we're ready.

\. means the decimal point; for example, $6.96.

\- is for a negative number. If a negative number is detected in the Data Merge, those numbers will appear in blue because you owe nothing and it will count as a credit on your next payment later.

So is that all you need to alter numbers? Well, not really. You can get even more technical if you want to.

Check out the next file: PriceMerge_End_2.indd. This file is basically the same except I've added a few more options to the Owe Price style for you to consider. Refer to Figure 6-64.

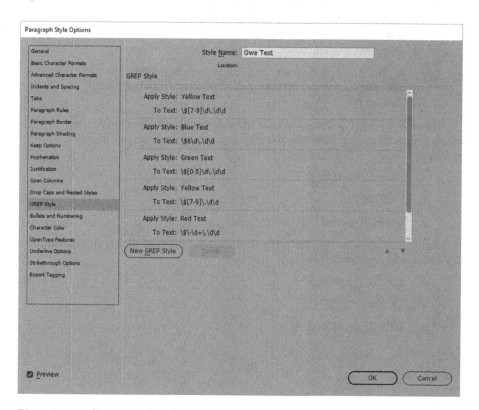

Figure 6-64. Alternate options for styling various ranges of text in a Data Merge

Look at these examples:

- \$(7-9)\d\.\d\d: Ranges from $70.00 to $99.99 could be another color.

- \$6\d\.\d\d: Ranges from $60.00 to 69.99 could be one color.

- \$(0-5)\d\.\d\d: Ranges from $10.00 to $59.99 could be another color.

- \$(0-9)\.\d\d: Ranges from $0.00 to $10.00 could be another color. Note that this slightly overrides another GREP.

- \$(?<=[\D])[0-9]\d{2,3}\.\d\d: This is for 2,3 digit numbers like $100.00 or $1000.00, by adding the {3} and {2} can affect which larger numbers will be affected.

If you're just working with numbers such as percentages or decimals, you don't need to use the dollar sign; just leave it out like this:

\d+\.\d\d

Here are some other examples:

- [6-9]\d|[\d]{3,}: This will style the numbers from 60 and up. This GREP code is a combination of two codes with an IF condition using a pipe sign (|).The second part, [\d]{3,}, will select all the digits with a minimum of three digits.

- [6-9]\d: Any digit from 6 to 9 followed by any digit. This code will select and search all the numbers starting with 6 and going through 9.

However, keep in mind that this code will also search and select the numbers in between bigger numbers, therefore, you must look for the numbers that are not preceded by a digit:

- (?<=[\D])[1-4]\d

- (?<=[\D])5\d

- (?<=[\D])[6-9]\d

Similarly, if you want to restrict your search to a two-or three-digit search string, you can add an additional code, like {1} or {2} or {3}:

- (?<=[\D])[1-4]\d{2}

- (?<=[\D])5\d{2}

- (?<=[\D])[6-9]\d{1}

■ **Note**   You can also use GREPs to find and search in your document. Go to Edit ➤ Find/
Change to open the Find/Change dialog box, shown in Figure 6-65. Make sure to check out
the links to resources provided if you want to learn more about out how this works.

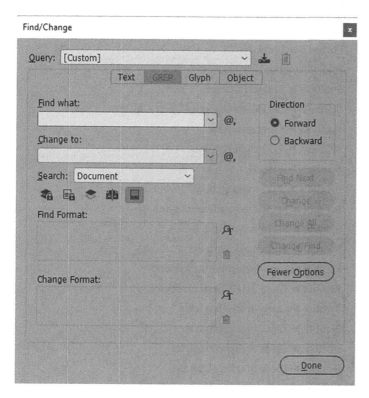

Figure 6-65. *You can use GREPs to find and change words while working in a document*

GREP Symbols

Note that all GREP symbols might not work with Data Merge text. Refer to Table 6-1.

Table 6-1. *Possible GREP Symbols Found Under the @ Symbol Icon and Where to Locate Them*

Symbol	Location/Name
\t	Tab
\n	Forced line break
\r	End of paragraph
~8	Symbols ➤ Bullet character
\\	Symbols ➤ Backslash character
\^	Symbols ➤ Caret character
~2	Symbols ➤ Copyright symbol
~e	Symbols ➤ Ellipsis
~7	Symbols ➤ Paragraph symbol
~r	Symbol ➤ Registered trademark symbol
~6	Symbol ➤ Section symbol
~d	Symbol ➤ Trademark symbol
\(	Symbol ➤ Open parenthesis character
\)	Symbol ➤ Close parenthesis character
\{	Symbol ➤ Open brace character
\}	Symbol ➤ Close brace character
\[	Symbol ➤ Open bracket character
\]	Symbol ➤ Close bracket character
~#	Markers ➤ Any page number
~N	Markers ➤ Current page number
~X	Markers ➤ Next page number
~V	Markers ➤ Previous page number
~x	Markers ➤ Section marker
~a	Markers ➤ Anchored object marker
~F	Markers ➤ Footnote reference marker
~U	Markers ➤ Endnote reference marker
~I	Markers ➤ Index marker
~_	Hyphens and Dashes ➤ Em dash
~=	Hyphens and Dashes ➤ En dash

(continued)

Table 6-1. (*continued*)

Symbol	Location/Name
~-	Hyphens and Dashes ➤ Discretionary hyphen
~~	Hyphens and Dashes ➤ Nonbreaking hyphen
~m	White Space ➤ Em space
~>	White Space ➤ En space
~f	White Space ➤ Flush space
~|	White Space ➤ Hair space
~S	White Space ➤ Nonbreaking space
~s	White Space ➤ Nonbreaking space (fixed width)
~<	White Space ➤ Thin space
~/	White Space ➤ Figure space
~.	White Space ➤ Punctuation space
~3	White Space ➤ Third space
~4	White Space ➤ Quarter space
~%	White Space ➤ Sixth space
"	Quotation Marks ➤ Any double quotation marks
'	Quotation Marks ➤ Any single quotation mark (apostrophe)
~"	Quotation Marks ➤ Straight double quotation marks
~{	Quotation Marks ➤ Double left quotation mark
~}	Quotation Marks ➤ Double right quotation mark
~'	Quotation Marks ➤ Straight single quotation mark (apostrophe)
~[	Quotation Marks ➤ Single left quotation mark
~]	Quotation Marks ➤ Single right quotation mark
~b	Break Character ➤ Standard carriage return
~M	Break Character ➤ Column break
~R	Break Character ➤ Frame break
~P	Break Character ➤ Page break
~L	Break Character ➤ Odd page break
~E	Break Character ➤ Even page break
~k	Break Character ➤ Discretionary line break
~v	Variable ➤ Any variable
~Y	Variable ➤ Running reader (paragraph style)
~Z	Variable ➤ Running header (character style)

(*continued*)

Table 6-1. (*continued*)

Symbol	Location/Name
~u	Variable ➤ Custom text
~T	Variable ➤ Last page number
~H	Variable ➤ Chapter number
~O	Variable ➤ Creation date
~o	Variable ➤ Modification date
~D	Variable ➤ Output date
~l	Variable ➤ File name
~J	Variable ➤ Metadata caption
~y	Other ➤ Right indent tab
~i	Other ➤ Indent to here
~h	Other ➤ End nested style here
~j	Other ➤ Nonjoiner
\d	Wildcards ➤ Any digit
[\l\u]	Wildcards ➤ Any letter
.	Wildcards ➤ Any character
\s	Wildcards ➤ Any white space
\w	Wildcards ➤ Any word character
\u	Wildcards ➤ Any uppercase letter
\l	Wildcards ➤ Any lowercase letter
\<	Locations ➤ Beginning of word
\>	Locations ➤ End of word
\b	Locations ➤ Word boundary
^	Locations ➤ Beginning of paragraph
$	Locations ➤ End of paragraph
?	Repeat ➤ Zero or one time
*	Repeat ➤ Zero or more times
+	Repeat ➤ One or more times
??	Repeat ➤ Zero or one time (shortest match)
*?	Repeat ➤ Zero or more times (shortest match)
+?	Repeat ➤ One or more times (shortest match)
()	Match ➤ Marking subexpression

(*continued*)

Table 6-1. (*continued*)

Symbol	Location/Name
(?:)	Match ➤ Nonmarking subexpression
[]	Match ➤ Character set
|	Match ➤ Or
(?<=)	Match ➤ Positive lookbehind
(?<!)	Match ➤ Negative lookbehind
(?=)	Match ➤ Positive lookahead
(?!)	Match ➤ Negative lookahead
(?i)	Modifiers ➤ Case-insensitive on
(?-i)	Modifiers ➤ Case-insensitive off
(?m)	Modifiers ➤ Multiline on
(?-m)	Modifiers ➤ Multiline off
(?s)	Modifiers ➤ Single-line on
(?-s)	Modifiers ➤ Single-line off
[[:alnum:]]	Posix ➤ [[:alnum:]]
[[:alpha:]]	Posix ➤ [[:alpha:]]
[[:digit:]]	Posix ➤ [[:digit:]]
[[:lower:]]	Posix ➤ [[:lower:]]
[[:punct:]]	Posix ➤ [[:punct:]]
[[:space:]]	Posix ➤ [[:space:]]
[[:upper:]]	Posix ➤ [[:upper:]]
[[:word:]]	Posix ➤ [[:word:]]
[[:xdigit:]]	Posix ➤ [[:xdigit:]]
[[==]]	Posix ➤ [[=a=]]

Summary

In this chapter, you learned about styling your Data Merge text with Paragraph and Character styles. You also incorporated GREP styles either as a word or a combination of metacharacters.

As you can, see GREPs can be complicated, but they can also be powerful styling tools for Data Merges or any InDesign project.

I hope that the chapters and projects I have provided in this session have been helpful.

The concluding chapter includes some troubleshooting tips and a quiz to test your knowledge of what you have learned in the previous chapters.

Troubleshooting

In this chapter, you'll look at a few troubleshooting tips to ensure that your InDesign Data Merge project runs smoother and conclude with a quiz to test your knowledge.

Note   If you want to work along in this lesson or review the result, download your Chapter 7 files from http://www.apress.com/9781484231586.

Putting Data Merge Fields on the Master Page

Throughout the book you might have noticed that two items on the Data Merge panel shortcut menu remained unavailable, as displayed in Figure 7-1: Update Content in Data Fields and Show Log of Update Results.

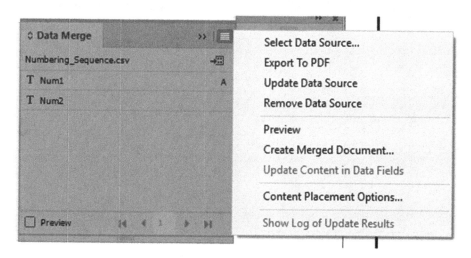

Figure 7-1. *Note the two items in the menu that have remained unavailable*

As mentioned, when you work with the Data Merge panel and you correct something in the `.csv` file, you can select Update Data Source.

When a data source is added the Data Merge panel, that same link will also show up in the Links panel, shown in Figure 7-2.

Figure 7-2. *The Links panel lists all the files that are linked, including .csv files*

To retain that link into the merged document, when you select Create Merged Document (e.g., `Letter1-1.indd`). You need to place your Data Merge field in a text box on the A-Master template (see Figure 7-3). Otherwise when you perform the merge, the data will still appear in the document but the original link will be lost, as shown in Figure 7-4.

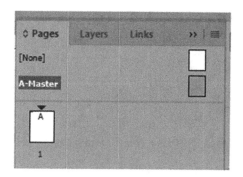

Figure 7-3. *In this example, rather than on page 1 even the data merge is added to the A-Master page*

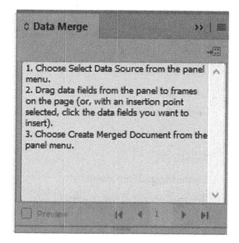

Figure 7-4. *The link is broken in the merge document if the Data Merge fields are not on the Master page when the merged document is created. Regardless, the data will still appear in the merge file*

■ **Note** In the lessons, I kept my Data Merge field on page 1 because I wanted the data merge to be accessible and not to interfere with stationary items on the Master page. However, if you find putting your data on a layer in the A-Master works better for your workflow, feel free to use this method to access the unavailable items in the created merged file, as shown in Figure 7-5.

Figure 7-5. *Whether you choose to keep the Data Merge fields on the A-Master or on page 1 you can stil keep them on a separate layer*

If you kept the data fields on the Master page, location shows up as an A rather than a number like 1. When the merged document is created, you will notice that besides the link being maintained, you can now select Update Content in Data Fields, shown in Figure 7-6.

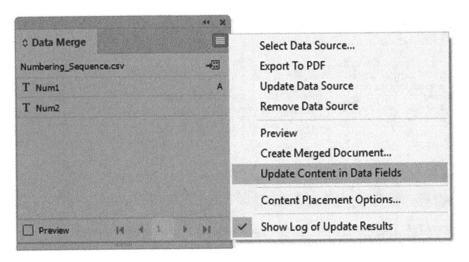

Figure 7-6. *The Update Content in Data Fields item is now available in the newly merged document*

If for some reason the data in your original .csv has changed and you select this menu item, you will receive the alert shown in Figure 7-7.

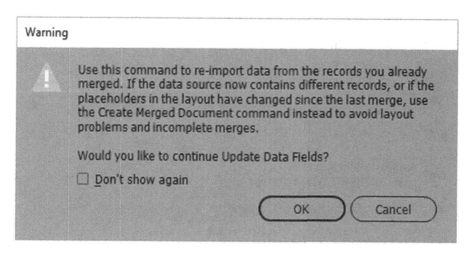

Figure 7-7. The alert that appears when Update Content in Data Fields is selected

If you have not altered anything other than some text in a field, click OK. Otherwise I would recommend going back to the original Data Merge file, selecting Update Data Source, and creating a new merged document.

You will also notice that in this merged document, whether Preview is turned on or off in the Data Merge panel, there will be a [ ] bracket around the fields, as depicted in Figure 7-8. This is to show that the link is still being maintained.

[001]   [<<Num1>>]

Figure 7-8. Notice that because the fields are on the A-Master in the merged file, the brackets around the fields indicate they have maintained their links

The Show Log of Update Results check box is also selected for the merged document. If this is selected, after you click OK to the Update Content in Data Fields, your computer might ask if you want to view the log. As shown in Figure 7-9, find an app like Notepad or Notepad++ and click OK.

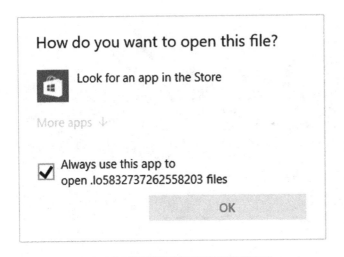

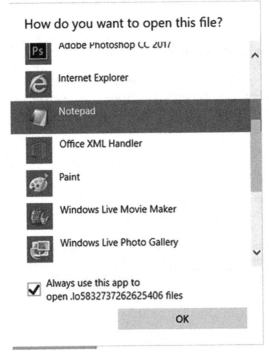

Figure 7-9. *Find a program in which you can view the log. I chose Notepad because it is just text*

You will be able to view the log in your text editor and it will read something like this:

```
Log of Update Data Fields.
Document Name:  Letter-1
Date of update: 2017-08-02
Data Source:    Numbering_Sequence.csv
There were no changes to the data source.
```

Or you might see:

```
Log of Update Data Fields.
Document Name:    Letter-1
Date of update:   2017-08-02
Data Source:      Numbering_Sequence.csv
Modified records: 1
Details:
Record 2 (key = autokey2) was modified.
```

If you don't want to see the log each time, make sure to clear this check box.

■ **Note**   Although I find this method does work okay for a single record merge with more than one text box, in the case of trying to merge multiple records, I did find that it acted a little buggy. Some of the records seemed to lose their brackets afterward when I updated the merged document. For multiple merges, I would recommend that you keep the merged text on page 1 rather than the A-Master. You will not be able to access the Update Content in Data Field option on the menu, but if you are exporting to PDF as in Chapter 5, this should make only a minor difference. You can always go back to the original Data Merge file and select Update Data Source and then select Export to PDF again.

Also putting your Data Merge fields on the A-Master will not work in the case of single records where the Data Merge fields might be on two or more pages, such as a longer letter or a booklet.

■ **Tip**   If you plan to put your Data Merge fields on a Master page, be aware that you should clear the Facing Pages check box when you create a new document, as shown in Figure 7-10.

If you do not clear this check box and you place your data on the left-hand page in the master rather than the right, the data merge will not show up because page 1 is always the right page. Therefore, to avoid confusion when you create a new file that will be a Data Merge, always clear the Facing Pages check box. That way only one sheet will show up for the A-Master page. Refer to Figures 7-11 and 7-12.

Figure 7-10. *Clear the Facing Pages check box when creating a file for the Data Merge*

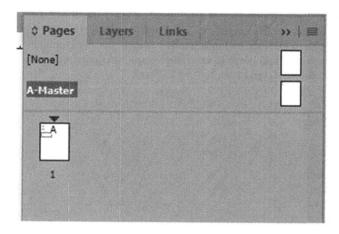

Figure 7-11. *How the Pages panel should appear when you start creating a Data Merge project*

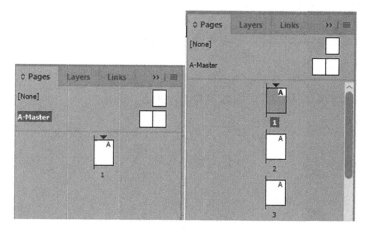

Figure 7-12. *If you select the Facing Pages check box when you create the InDesign document and put your date on the A-Master as in the left image, be aware what the result will be when you create a merge document: Only data on the right appears and you lose the left data*

Additional Troubleshooting Tips

If your field in the .csv file contains a comma, as in MyCompany, Ltd., be aware that this might in some cases cause InDesign CC to think that this is another field rather than a comma that is part of the text field. If this does happen, go back to the .csv file and put double straight quotes around the word like this: "MyCompany, Ltd." Resave the file, and then it should be recognized as one field.

On the Options tab of the Create Merge Document dialog box, do not set the Record Limit per Document or Page Limit per Document settings to one page, as this could slow down the program or cause it to crash. Rather, it is better to leave it at a reasonable number like 20 or 50 or leave these check boxes cleared (see Figure 7-13) and then separate the files in Adobe Acrobat DC Pro as you saw in Chapter 3.

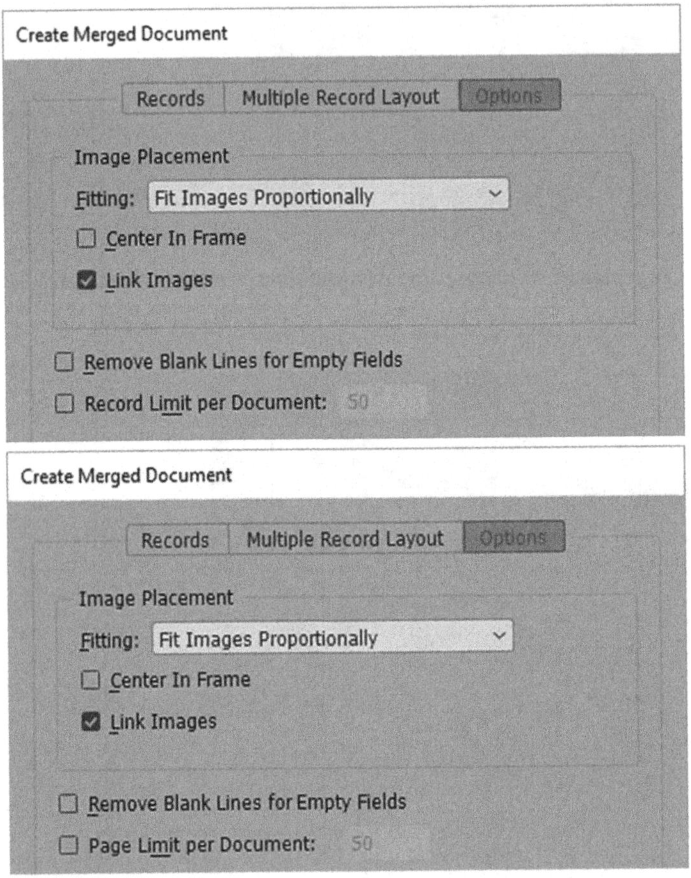

Figure 7-13. *For single record (top) or multiple records (bottom), either leave the limits per document settings cleared to run the full merge or set a reasonable range*

If you have created several merged records and exported them as PDFs at separate times you can easily combine them all later as one file in Acrobat DC Pro.

Simply select all the records in your Chapter 7 folder, right-click and on the shortcut menu select Combine Files in Acrobat, as shown in Figure 7-14.

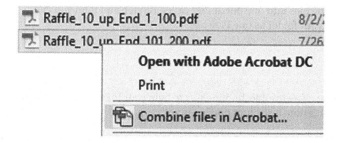

Figure 7-14. *Combine your files in Adobe Acrobat*

Acrobat will then open and allow you to combine all the files. Just drag with your mouse to reorder if you must adjust the order and then click Combine in the upper right as displayed in Figure 7-15.

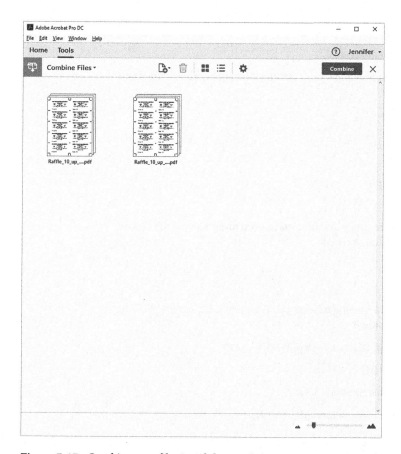

Figure 7-15. *Combine your files in Adobe Acrobat using the Combine Files tool*

259

Acrobat will combine the files into one document called Binder, and then you can rename and save this file in your folder as one PDF file.

Summary

In this chapter, you looked at a few troubleshooting tips to help your InDesign Data Merge project run smoother. Now it's time test your knowledge with a quiz.

Quiz: Test Your Knowledge

Here is a final quiz to test your knowledge of Data Merges.

1. What area should you reset each time you plan to work on a Data Merge project?

    a. Preferences

    b. Workspace

    c. Document Presets

2. Which of the following styles can affect the appearance of the Data Merge?

    a. Character

    b. Cell

    c. Object

    d. Paragraph

    e. Table

3. You can create single and multiple record merges using the Data Merge panel and its menu.

    a. True

    b. False

4. Which of the following formats can InDesign CC not use to link the Data Merge panel?

    a. CSV UTF-8 (Comma delimited) (*.csv)

    b. Excel Workbook (*.xlsx)

    c. Text Tab delimited (*.txt)

    d. CSV (Comma delimited) (*.csv)

5. What symbol should you use in your `.csv` file's field heading to indicate that the links will be for images?

   a. #Photos

   b. @Photos

   c. *Photos

6. What symbol should you use in your `.csv` file's field heading to indicate that the data will be for a QR code?

   a. #Qrcode

   b. @Qrcode

   c. *Qrocde

7. You can drag fields from the Data Merge panel into a table.

   a. True

   b. False

8. If you want to create sequential numbering without using the Data Merge panel, which tab do you need to format in your Paragraph Style Options dialog box?

   a. General

   b. Indents and Spacing

   c. Bullets and Numbering

9. Which tab in the Paragraph Style Options dialog box can you use to alter the color of your text depending on the name in a Title style during the Data Merge?

   a. Character Color

   b. GREP Styles

   c. Advanced Character Formatting

10. Which tab of the Paragraph Style Options dialog box allows you to override some of the formatting of other Character styles that were applied elsewhere on another tab?

    a. Character Color

    b. GREP Styles

    c. Drop Caps and Nested Styles

11. You can use the Based On setting on the General tab in either Paragraph or Character styles to quickly copy settings from an earlier style.

    a. True

    b. False

12. When you create a document for a Data Merge it should not have facing pages.

    a. True

    b. False

13. In the Data Merge panel, what are the two dialog boxes that you can use to edit how your inline images will display?

    a. ＿＿＿＿＿＿

    b. ＿＿＿＿＿＿

14. When you export to PDF from a Data Merge file you enter what dialog box before you reach the Export to PDF dialog box?

    a. Content Placement Options

    b. Create Merged Document

    c. Select Data Source

15. If you change some data in a field in your .csv file and then save and close it, what menu item should you choose from InDesign Data Merge panel?

    a. Select Data Source

    b. Update Data Source

    c. Remove Data Source

16. When you create a multiple record merge in InDesign, where is the check box located that allows you to preview the records to make sure they are laid out correctly?

    a. Data Merge panel ➤ Preview

    b. Create Merged Document dialog box ➤ Preview when Records per Document Page is set to Single Record.

    c. Create Merged Document dialog box ➤ Preview when Records per Document Page is set to Multiple Records.

17. Data Merge projects can have more than one Master page.

    a. True

    b. False

18. If you wanted to create a frame background (nondata merge item) for your images with a drop shadow and a gradient, which tool could you use to do both in the same dialog box?

    a. Object Styles panel

    b. Gradient panel

    c. Effects panel

19. Data Merge text can be on its own layer whether inside or outside of the Page Master.

    a. True

    b. False

20. To highlight the Data Merge text field use:

    a. Selection tool

    b. Type tool

    c. Direct Selection tool

Answers

1. b

2. a and d

3. a

4. a and b

5. b

6. a

7. a

8. c

9. b

10. c

11. a

12. a

13. a. Create Merged Document; b. Content Placement Options

14. b

15. b

16. c

17. b

18. a

19. a

20. b

Index

© Jennifer Harder 2017
J. Harder, *Data Merge and Styles for Adobe InDesign CC 2018*,
https://doi.org/10.1007/978-1-4842-3159-3

Get the eBook for only $5!

Why limit yourself?

With most of our titles available in both PDF and ePUB format, you can access your content wherever and however you wish—on your PC, phone, tablet, or reader.

Since you've purchased this print book, we are happy to offer you the eBook for just $5.

To learn more, go to http://www.apress.com/companion or contact support@apress.com.

Apress®

All Apress eBooks are subject to copyright. All rights are reserved by the Publisher, whether the whole or part of the material is concerned, specifically the rights of translation, reprinting, reuse of illustrations, recitation, broadcasting, reproduction on microfilms or in any other physical way, and transmission or information storage and retrieval, electronic adaptation, computer software, or by similar or dissimilar methodology now known or hereafter developed. Exempted from this legal reservation are brief excerpts in connection with reviews or scholarly analysis or material supplied specifically for the purpose of being entered and executed on a computer system, for exclusive use by the purchaser of the work. Duplication of this publication or parts thereof is permitted only under the provisions of the Copyright Law of the Publisher's location, in its current version, and permission for use must always be obtained from Springer. Permissions for use may be obtained through RightsLink at the Copyright Clearance Center. Violations are liable to prosecution under the respective Copyright Law.

Printed in the United States
By Bookmasters